I Ain't Nobody's
Negro

I Ain't Nobody's
Negro

The Black Man's Struggle for Life,
Liberty, and Justice Around the World

Dr. Akeam Amoniphis Simmons

I AIN'T NOBODY'S NEGRO
THE BLACK MAN'S STRUGGLE FOR LIFE, LIBERTY, AND JUSTICE AROUND THE WORLD

iUniverse books may be ordered through booksellers or by contacting:

iUniverse
1663 Liberty Drive
Bloomington, IN 47403
www.iuniverse.com
1-800-Authors (1-800-288-4677)

Because of the dynamic nature of the Internet, any web addresses or links contained in this book may have changed since publication and may no longer be valid. The views expressed in this work are solely those of the author and do not necessarily reflect the views of the publisher, and the publisher hereby disclaims any responsibility for them.

Any people depicted in stock imagery provided by Getty Images are models, and such images are being used for illustrative purposes only.
Certain stock imagery © Getty Images.

ISBN: 978-1-5320-5984-1 (sc)
ISBN: 978-1-5320-5985-8 (e)

Print information available on the last page.

iUniverse rev. date: 10/08/2018

Mama

I will always remember mama's words just before she chastised me: "Um whipping you so that the white man won't have to because he won't whip you with love." What profound wisdom mama had, for she knew the hard cold injustice that lay ahead for her son. She tried to prepare me as best she could.

To Jehovah
My creator and sustainer-The Most High God

All Bible passages within the proceeding pages are taken
from the King James interpretation of the Bible

Contents

I am black, but comely, O you daughters of Jerusalem, as the tents of Kedar, as the curtains of Solomon.

Look not upon me, because I am black, because the sun has looked upon me; my mother's children were angry with me; they made me the keeper of the vineyards; but my own vineyard have I not kept.

THE SONG OF SOLOMON 1: 5-6

THE NEGRO

Before we journey any further in this expose' that is dealing with the struggles of the black people through injustice, racialism, and rampant pervading discrimination, we must give a definitive description to the word and term Negro, for the word encapsulates great ignorance and ambiguities even amongst black people.

-The dictionary defines Negro as- a member of a dark-skinned group of people originally native to Africa south of the Sahara.

Quoted from the Oxford dictionary

-A word relating to black people.

Quoted from Google definition

-Definition of Negro, plural Negros, dated, now sometimes offensive; a member of a race of humankind native to Africa and classified according to physical features (such as dark skin pigmentation)

Quoted from Merriam-Webster dictionary

Notice, none of the dictionaries related the word Negro to slavery-recorded history is always flavored by the penman.

The word Negro was first used by the Portuguese which was the Spanish word for black, but as the dark skinned man travelled further into North

America, the word Negro developed a negative connotation-The North Americans gave the word Negro to mean more than just black; they connected it to his humanity; to them, the Negro was lower than, or equal to just another lower life animal that was designed to serve the white man as slave or indentured servant, or as a share cropper, which was dressed up slavery.

The word Negro was used more in the 1900, particularly during the 1950's, than any other time, even more than from the 1600 through the 1800, because it was during the 1900s that the black man struggled the most to attain his rights and freedom, and to truly become an American citizen and the right to be counted as a man, and be "included", and not treated as an animal. The term Negro expressly refers to the black slave.

When one studies African ethnicities and tribes, one will find many different kinds of tribes- over 3000 ethnic groups, and over 2000 different languages.

Some of the tribes were:

The Maasai tribe of Kenya and Tanzania

The Himba tribe of Numibia

The Kunda of tribe of Zambia

The Samburn tribe of Kenya

The San Bushmen tribe of Batswana

The Xhosa tribe of South Africa

The Zulu tribe of South Africa

The tusi tribe

The Pygmies tribes

But, the tribes that most of the slaves of North America came from are most likely from West Africa-the Ghana region; such as the:

The Ashuti tribe

The Berber tribe

The Dogan tribe

The Dinka tribe

The Fang tribe

Note, I have yet to find any tribe called Negro, though they are all black tribes, because there is none. Of the over 12.5 million slaves, none were from a tribe called Negro; no, that is the name given to the slaves by their captors; deriding any thoughts of him being any more that a piece of property, a commodity with which they used and abused and then tossed it aside amongst their other used up commodities.

So, every time that the white folks referred to the black man as Negro, it reminded him and them of "who" he was supposed to be-less than them and beneath them-the white man-a piece of property that has lost its value to its owner.

The North Americans were the ones that gave "the Negro name" the degrading and offensive nature-to be referred to as Negro was humiliating, and "Nigger", is simply a derivative of Negro-a more degrading way of referring to a black man as a Negro; which is the reason why I cannot understand why would any logical or learned black man refer to himself or his brothers as Nigger. For a black man to refer to himself as Nigger, implies that he has accepted the North American's definition and description of himself and his race as less than human.

Thus, "Negro" as a name for a people was birth from the slave trade; an humiliated, degraded group of people that was treated less than animals and were merely a piece of property owned by the white man. A freed ex-slave was still called Negro because he used to be owned by the white man.

HENCE, I AIN'T NOBODY'S NEGRO -NO MORE

I am a black man; the pigment of my skin is dark because my ancestors were of African descent, and lived their lives bathing beneath the richness of Jehovah's golden sun.

Negro is not an African word; it didn't derive from Africa. So now, I refuse to refer to myself by something that those that abhorred me gave unto my people.

And, I can never understand why some blacks refer to themselves by something that the white slave master gave unto them denoting white property, or worst still referring to themselves as Nigger-somebody's property, an even more demeaning term inferred upon the black man- what gross ignorance.

I am of African descent that was born and raised in America-thus, I am African American that is due and owed all of the rights, liberties, and privileges given to any and all Americans.

I can no more deny Africa, as I cannot deny America, for both of them run richly through my veins. My great great grandparents were ripped from Africa and forced into America, and so I and my generations were born and raised in America-thus, we know nothing of Africa, saving that is where our forefathers were ripped from.

I am American and African through and through; I cannot deny either, for I am both wrapped in one beneath my rich dark skin.

Sometimes it is as though I have no home, for the Africans think that I am not truly African, even though I have African blood running richly through my veins- they are partly right; and America says that I am not truly American because I was taken from Africa.

So, I go wounded by both of my heritages that refused to accept me.

I am both, African and American, for both develop my rich heritage that is filled with hurt, pain, pride, and confusion. I am not now nor ever have been "a Negro", for I have never been a slave; nor

my mother or father, nor my grandparents, so we were born free Americans whose skin is black and heritage is that of Africa.

Although many black men are free, and have never been a slave, they still, none-the-less, possess the Negro mentality. They still want to be just like Mr. Charlie, so they dye their hair, color their eyes, fight against other blacks, and often live beyond their means, and expect Mr. Charlie to come into their neighborhoods and make them safe, and expect the white man to take care of the children that they have left behind and refused to parent because they are adamantly trying to be as white as they can.

The black race, as a people, must pull off that Negro character and mentality, for as long as we possess that mentality, we will never rise up and achieve or possess their God given freedom, or acquiesce their lawful American citizenship and rights.

We, the black race, must embrace who we truly are-black African Americans; and though not all of us are descendants of kings and queens, many of us are.

We must come face to face with the fact that no one of any other race, or country is willing to help us more than we are willing to help ourselves; which is the reason why we can no more afford ourselves to remain a Negro, but we must truly walk in our real identify of African American-still fighting and struggling to ascertain our full rights of American citizen with equal rights just as any other American citizen.

Letter of love filled with forgiveness

To the slave master-then and now

Forgiveness is so powerful because one has to "choose" to forgive even while one's heart is still broken, and tears are screaming down your cheeks, and the memories of the offence is yet alive.

To my white and mixed perpetrators where ever they might be around the world, particularly those of the North American soil.

Though you have caused me undue hurt and harm, and have over and over again denied me life, liberty, and justice, things for which you automatically give to your children and others whose pigment is of your own, I forgive you and love you still; for I know that I cannot become all that I can be unless I forgive you for all that you have done to me. I love you with a Godly love and forgiveness.

Let it be known to all men, both at home and abroad, I forgive you for denying me the rights to a full life; I forgive you for all the lynching that you carried out relentlessly upon my fathers, and the endless rapes you straddled my mothers, sisters, and daughters with-a rape that watered down my black color and infused me with your blood to whereby some of my children now have olive skin, gray eyes, and straight hair.

I forgive you for forcing my fathers to work your fields, cook your meals, raise your children without pay, and forcing my people to be indentured servants and share croppers to ease your own conscience while at the very same time continuing to increase your wealth through painted slavery.

I forgive you for stealing my Identity and wiping away my heritage and name, and forcing me to accept your name and your culture.

I forgive you for making my black skin abhorred around the world-to such an extent that foreigners demonize and criminalize me even before ever even knowing me-my only criminal offence is being born blackl.

I forgive you for not including me in your constitutions and bill of rights, and I forgive you for not keeping the rights for which you did write for me.

I forgive you for being too liberal to do me any good or help my cause, even though you fully beheld the injustice forced upon me and my children.

And, I love you still, though I am aware that you still deny me life, liberty and justice; I love you still, though I know that you continue to ravage my neighborhoods, and send my fathers and sons to prison.

I love you with a Godly love and will not give up on you.

I forgive you, and hope and pray that someday we can become great together and live as equals; where someday we can sit down at the table of brotherly love and commune with each other.

I forgive because I know that in order for me to fully reach the destiny that God has for me, I must forgive you of all the wrong doings and injustices perpetrated against me and my people.

My people have been ravaged from one end of the globe to the other, and because of this, many of us fail to realize who we are, so we adopt your ways, your character, and your psychological thinking, and it silently leads us to hate ourselves and anybody that looks like us.

You confused us, but I forgive you and love you still.

I love you enough to hope that someday you shall honor your laws written for all men regardless of race, creed, or color. I love you enough to believe that soon God shall invade your heart and afford you the ability to see us as equals-though the pigment of our skin be different, none-the-less, equals to stand, live, and fight together in a common cause that enhance all of us-human-kind.

A POEM

I Am An American

They say that I am an American
But they don't treat me like I am an American
I was born in America
But the constitution wasn't written for me
Or people like me

I am too dark you see
To be part of the brave and the free
I am the American they wish to hide
The America they don't pride
The America where my slave bearing fathers cried

I built their roads
Their fields I hoed
And from sun up till sun down I carried their load
While their clothes I sowed
Forever traveling down that lonely road
Of hoping to be an American before sold

I want to be an American
A black American
Or yellow American
Or brown American

But still an American

Where I can be part of the revolution
And help strengthen the American constitution
I need not promised restitution
But free me from unfairly imprisoned institution

I am an American through and through
I didn't just appear here like the morning dew
But I was born and raised here by somebody they knew
Somebody they long ago slew
With their club bearing noose hanging crew

I fought on both sides of the civil war
Not fully understanding what I was fighting for
I had to push slavery ajar
Never to accept it even from afar
I am an American the proof is in my deep riddled scar

Oh I am proud of red white and blue
Though not so proud of some of the things that we do
Even when I am discriminated because of my black skin's hue
In my heart I'll not let hatred brew
Because I am an American that's what we do

I am an American through and through
Red white and blue
Many flee other nations to come here too
But they are not Americans through and through
1776 we started anew
And 1866 they grafted me in too
Now I am an American just like you

So I vote
And the ballad I tote
Because in America opinions float

And surround the White House like a moat

I am an American recognize me
And allow me to be
The American I long for you to see
An American that was born free
To help this country become as great as it can be

I am an American

Foreword

First allow me to disclaim any prematurely conceived, or misconceived thoughts or prejudices in or about this expose' where I attempt, no matter how futile, to bring a degree of clarity to our cause, our struggles, and our discontentment that overwhelmingly plague the black race simply because of the color of our skin.

This book is not about the white man, though he causes black people an endless amount of grief and sorrow. It is about the black people and how we can better ourselves and be the best that God created us to be. The struggle is about us-black people. It is about pulling off the subservient man boy that the white folks created for themselves-the Negro.

Too, I don't assert, in any way or tone, that all white men are bad, though, I've been denied life, liberty, and justice by him all of my life, and though, I've never met a white man that could look pass the color of my skin, and I don't rightly know whether I'd want him to either, for I am proud of this black pigment that invades my epidermis skin from a subcutaneous implantation given me by my very black forefathers. I still refuse to believe that all white men are bad.

As a matter of fact, I love my white brother too; not with a feigned kind of love, but a pure Godly kind love; a love that sees the best in my brother, and sees the best in me.

And, because of this agape love that only can come from God, I forgive my white brother for gross mistreatment; I forgive him for the many lynchings, the beatings, and the degradation and deprivation that he constantly forces upon me and my brothers-most of us even from birth.

In perhaps a strange kind of way, I understand my white brothers; for maybe if I was the majority race and atop the economical latter, perhaps I too would become narcissistic and suffer solipsism to where I began to think that I am better than people that are not my color.

I understand that it is most difficult for anybody or any group of people to be filled with humility when they have so much-it is, perhaps, human nature.

I forgive my white brother though for denying me the rights and privileges promised to me in his laws and constitution as an American. I love him still.

There is good in all men, but that for which we, as mere mortal men, display the most is what we become apparently known for.

And, because I have come to realize that black injustice permeates the globe at large, I include my brothers and sisters of color everywhere across the globe filled with human kind. **We weep for and with each other.**

So it is with my white brothers that my passions reckon with, for he has ravaged Africa, enslaved its citizens, and brought its children to a land of injustice where he refused to acknowledge their God given rights of freedom, justice, and life.

So, this expose' attempts to unveil some of our causes, and reactions, so that those that truly want to understand us and assist us can.

And, at the end of the day, after all has been said and done, we, black and white, need each other; we are better together than we are apart.

We must pick our swords up, and embrace our differences, and march down the halls of injustice, and fight together hand in hand. Our causes must become one; our fight must become "our" fight, and not "their" fight.

Injustice is a cancer; if gone untreated, it will kill everything in its path, and threaten every fiber of justice everywhere.

Because we, both black and white, make up the main, we are both effected by that which ails and stricken the main; so, as the great poet John Donne pinned in part: Ask not for whom the bell tolls. The bell tolls for thee.

My situation is your situation, and your situation is mine. The degree of melanin in my skin does not define who I am; it does not readily identify me; it simply quietly asserts that some of my ancestors lived a great deal of their lives in the sun.

So, I press forward in this book, hoping to give some degree of light to a cause of a people, black people that have been and continue to be denied life, liberty, justice, and the pursuit of happiness.

When it is all said and done, we all want the same things for ourselves and our families; that is the same desires inhabited by all men, nations, and countries.

We want the opportunity to do well and we want our children to have the same opportunity to aspire to achieve without undue prejudice.

But, we already know all too well that our greatest task is to teach the black man to pull off the Negro mentality, for the Negro is often as a docile creature that though he has been set free, he will oftentimes wonder willingly back to his familiar environment.

Introduction

I sit in the silence of the moment, staring out over the rolling sloping hills of Alabama, and I ponder deeply of all the rising tension at home and abroad.

So many world leaders are now easily spitting out bellicose rhetoric. It readily appears that most are trying desperately to emulate the tough guy disposition.

Deep down into the most secret canals of my mind, I hope and I pray that this will soon pass; for I know all too well that the ones that shall soon suffer the most from this renewed prejudice uprising will be people of color- my people.

The masses of us don't seem to see it or realize it. They are drawn into a fight that somebody else wanted and started, but penned the streamline on us- Knowing full well that the black man is already smitten by suffering from the harden grips of injustice; so he is that much easier to be coerce into another fight started by the white man for the white man.

We are sitting on a ticking time bomb that is ready to explode in a minute, right in our faces, but what most whites fail to realize is that it shall blow up in both our faces, ours and theirs, for we are no longer merely the passive people of yesterday, just hoping and praying that our misguided Caucasian brothers will wake up, rise up and treat us right and fairly.

No, this is a new generation- A generation that has tasted the sweet nectar of freedom, liberty, and justice for all-a generation that has gotten a whiff of equality and social retribution; a generation that has studied the Declaration of Independence and The Constitution and believes that they are, or should be a part of the "we the people".

The black millennials and black generation X have thrust their souls into the hymns of the apron of lady justice, and they refuse to be patient and wait any longer. No, they are not like their forefathers-just hope and pray that God will soon change our adversary and give him a heart to treat us fairly- and even, perhaps, learn to love us.

The black Millennials and the black generation X groups are the "right now" generation who wants tomorrow today, and wants everything that is owed to them given to them right now-laden with interest.

No, they refuse to sit and hope that they shall be given their share. They have been taught and trained that it is their right, and that they deserve it right now; so they, without hesitation, display the "entitlement" disposition- even to their own parents, and then society. They have evolved passed the forty acres and a mule that their forefathers were promised.

Their thought process now is, give us justice, freedom, and equality, and we will by our own forty acres of land, and they can keep the mule.

And, I can't altogether say that I blame them, for we have been waiting for far too long, and wait always means never; so, as the age old question protrudes, If not now, then when, and "when" in the black community is right now.

We seem to appear to no longer hunger and chase after that illusive wonder called justice, peace, love, equality, and cooperation. No, the mentality now is to annihilate anyone at the expense of everyone.

And, at the very heart of all of this confusion, tension, and fight, is the Negro, African American, Black man, or whatever you choose to call him-the man of color, or call yourself. The man of color is at the heart of the matter (when I say man, I am not meaning gender specific-male and female).

Some will quickly assert that racial tension has grown, but I beg to differ. It has not grown any more or less; it is the same that it has always been; it is just more quickly exposed than before because of social media and things of that sort.

News is now instantaneous; we can see it while it is happening or just after it happens.

Racial discrimination never went away; they made laws to force them to conceal it a little bit better. Instead of blatant hangings or lynchings or mobbings, and bursting into the front door; now, it still goes on, but they just use the back door, and their lynching now is more with the pen than with the rope; though the rope has not entirely been done away with.

Before I journey any further in this monologue, first, allow me to apologize if here after, I should seem too abrasive, crude, or rude. It is not my intensions to demean, dishonor, or lessen any man; however, I have chose to embrace the truth, no matter how bitter or distasteful it might be, or shall become for us and them, for truth is oftentimes distasteful.

History, as is, pure, simple and to the point, truthful history is often times abrasive; for if written as it occurred, it is shameful and hurtful to some and rightfully embarrassing to others. However, History is just that-history.

It is the recording of what transpired here-to-fore; and as such, history refuses to make some of our ancestor look too good and gracious, and sometimes makes some of them seem downright wicket and evil, but it is still, none-the-less, history-our history both black and white, intertwined together as one-thus, I am incomplete without you, and you are incomplete without me-like a fabric sown together, we are but an empty hole without each other.

Thus, is the reason why I cannot understand the logic behind the people that are determined to pull down statues of Confederate soldiers. It is history; a history that tells the Confederates that they lost.

Every time one sees a statue of Robert E. Lee and the likes, it should remind one of who lost the battle between the North and the South. It is only a statue of praise or glory in the eyes of the beholder.

I cannot tell you what you see, nor can you tell me what I see; to the one it signifies victory and defeat; to another, it signifies the will to fight, inspite of the terrible lost, but still truth lies within the very marble of which it stands.

Just because you tear down the statue doesn't mean that you wiped out history. So, I often want to ask, with that logic, what shall we do next, go in the history books and tear out anything and all pages that have to do with the ugliness of the south towards its black citizen?

No, because it is history; and if we are to make a better future, it is imperative that we learn from our past-history.

And so, here-to-with, we thrust our pen into the sandy banks of time that is filled with blackened, marred, and sometimes ugly by- gone events; some, that simply make us drop our heads and wonder why, and at the very same time, others, that make us lift our heads up in pride and marvel at the strength and resolve of our beloved forefathers-both black and white.

Too, it is almost impossible to get true and real and uncut history; for history is so often colored by the penman that poured his thoughts upon so fragile of paper and flavored it with his own pre-battered taste.

But, I shall forge ahead with a quest to stick to truth and right, even when it hurts and embarrasses the one that is reeling the ambiguous sword of the pen that spews out the ravenous ink upon unforgiving pages crested upon time immortal.

So, I leap forward as a lad amidst puberty, trying to fill the pages that fill the pages that be already full of flavored beguiled penmen.

Still, I leap forward with the sword of my pen sharpened and anxious to spew out the rich red blood of history; both black and white, so intertwined, that they seem as one.

P.S. For the sake of clarity, for future references, when I say in a text "Mr. Charlie", I am alluding to the white man; though, like us, he is called by many names, I refer to the name that gripped me most during my formative years-Mr. Charlie!

Chapter One

A Disenfranchised People

History is many times diluted and polluted with the interest of hidden parties and often inflated by the purse of the wealthy that simply buy the pages of bygone events.

Note the very beginning of "America".

The record says that Christopher Columbus discovered America in 1492, but it was already inhabited by native Indians, and if, in fact, Columbus had truly discovered the new world, why then was it named after Amerigo Vespucci in 1502-almost twelve years later.

I am not saying that Columbus did or did not discover the new world in 1492; I am merely emphasizing the point that an historical pen favored Amerigo Vespucci when recording the new world on the map.

Almost an hundred and twenty years later, in 1620 the pilgrims landed in Plymouth Rock Massachusetts. Some say for religious freedom, for that, I suppose, sounds more admirable, but that is not entirely true.

Yes, the pilgrims left England in search of religious freedom, but that led them to Leiden Holland where they acquired religious freedom. What led them to North America, Plymouth Rock Massachusetts, was because they felt that Leiden Holland was not a good place to raise their children and it was also a hard place to make a living-thus, they took sail to the new world of North America.

I submitted the voyages of Christopher Columbus and the Pilgrims to display the plight of the African black man who is so commonly referred to as the Negro.

Both voyages had slaves to help with Columbus and the Pilgrims arduously dangerous travels-even though history records slavery as starting in 1619.

1619 was simply the date that the slave became more of a commodity in North America; when they publicized the first African slaves in Jamestown Virginia to aid in the growth and harvest of tobacco, they unveiled a new lucrative commodity of cheap human labor-the slave.

England dispatched an entourage of Englanders to colonize the New World-North America, but England's greed caused them to over tax the colonies which led to colonial revolt, hence, taxation without representation. They were taxing them without taking fully good care of them.

Thus the colonies revolted and separated themselves, with their slaves amongst them, and sent the king of Great Britain a letter called the Declaration Of Independence. This document is important for Black people to note. Observe what it says, in part:

THE DECLARATION OF INDEPENDENCE

Congress, July 4, 1776.

When in the course of human events, it becomes necessary for one people to dissolve the political bands which have connected them with another, and to assume among the powers of the earth, the separate and equal station to which the laws of Nature and of Nature's God entitle them, a decent respect to the opinions of mankind requires that they should declare the causes which impel them to the separation.

We hold these truths to be self-evident, that all men are created equal, that they are endowed by their Creator with certain unalienable Rights, that among these are Life, Liberty, and the pursuit of Happiness.—That to secure these rights, Governments are instituted among Men, deriving their just powers from the consent of the governed,--That whenever any Form of Government becomes destructive of these ends, it is the Right of the People to alter or to abolish it, and to institute new Government, laying its foundation on such principles and organizing its powers in such form, as to them shall seem most likely to effect their Safety and Happiness. Prudence, indeed, will dictate that Governments long established should not be changed for light and transient causes; and accordingly all experience hath shewn, that mankind are more disposed to suffer, while evils are sufferable, than to right themselves by abolishing the forms to which they are accustomed. But when a long train of abuses and usurpations, pursuing

invariably the same Object evinces a design to reduce them under absolute Despotism, it is their right, it is their duty, to throw off such Government, and to provide new Guards for their future security.—Such has been the patient sufferance of these Colonies; and such is now the necessity which constrains them to alter their former Systems of Government.........
etc......etc......etc.

The above transcript is the United States Declaration of Independence in part.

Now, it Is crystal clear why the black people are a disenfranchised people-even now.

People of color was not intended to be included in The Declaration of Independence; for note specifically what The Declaration says, in part, in its second paragraph:

We hold these truths to be self-evident, that all men are created equal, that they are endowed by their Creator with certain unalienable Rights, that among these are Life, Liberty and the pursuit of Happiness.

WHAT? They wrote that their truth is self-evident, all men are equal and have been given by God certain unalienable Rights, and amongst the Rights are Life, Liberty, and the pursuit of Happiness.

But, they didn't mean that the black men were equal to them, and that the black man was due the right to pursue happiness and expect Liberty and a full Life; No, they were talking about all white folk, and they were not even including those white folk that had some black blood in them, for they believed that if one had just two percent of black blood in them, then they were considered black.

The black man is disenfranchised, deprived of rights, power, and therefore has no protection by the law from illegal mistreatment.

Yes, he is disenfranchised because he was never connected legally to the young country, even though the black man labored in their fields; hoed their crops, picked their cotton, built their roads, and constructed their big plantations where he never found any sense of justice.

Too, the black woman was never connected either; she too was treated like one of the animals on the farm. She washed Mr. Charlie's clothes, and then ironed them, cooked his food, scrubbed his floors, and raised his children, and even sometimes against her own will, she birth the white man some children after he had raped her on numerous occasion-even when her black husband knew about it, but was powerless to do anything because just like his wife, he was Mr. Charlie's property to do with as he pleased.

Sometimes the black man would sit on the porch of the shack that the white man had given him and his family to live in, and listen angrily at the white master while he forced himself upon his wife.

Yes, the end result of the white man raping the black women, is the variation of the color of our skin-hence, why some blacks are so light skinned, and come in different shades of color.

The black woman had the white man's children, and then was forced to raise them to be slaves-Because both of them were the white man's property.

When the settlers of the colony broke from England to become a free sovereign people, and develop their own country, they were not including the black slaves among them.

The Declaration of Independence was about the white man and his descendants.

Black people were disenfranchised because from the start of this country, they were not included.

So, the question is would the white people in the new colony, that just started a new country, would they change their behavior if given another chance?

When the citizens and new elected officials saw and realized that their country was not working as well as it needed to, they devised another plan; so you would think that they would include the black man in this new plan, seeing that even their old laws declares that "all men" created equal and are due certain rights, such as liberty, justice, and the pursuit of happiness, but they failed to include the blacks amongst them.

So, you would think that if they had to do it again, that perhaps, this time, they would include "all men" both whites and blacks.

Eleven years later, in 1787, they wrote a collection of laws for their young nation- They called it the constitution of the United States.

Note, how it too started, riddled in equal rights and justice for all-all but the black people among them.

Look what it says:

The Constitution of the United States

We the people of the United States, in order to form a more perfect union, establish justice, insure domestic tranquility, provide for the common defense, promote the general welfare, and secure the blessings of liberty to ourselves and our posterity, do ordain and establish this Constitution for the United States of America.

When they wrote, We the people of the United States, they were not including people of color, particularly the black man.

Again, just as in the Declaration of Independence, they write in the Constitution that Justice, tranquility, liberty, and wellbeing for all as an important issue.

Again, they were forming laws for them, the white man, Mr. Charlie and his offspring, not the black citizens and their offspring.

So thus, is the reason why the black man is disenfranchised, even now; because he was never intended to be included in the main of the United States.

When you have a people that have been stripped of economical strength, stripped of political strength, and stripped of social strength, you will systematically have a disenfranchised people.

Hence, is the reason why the black race and all people of color must increase their economical, social, and political strength.

Building ourselves up in theses area will make things better for ourselves and our posterity here-to-with.

Though, I must admit that it appears that most of the other races of people that migrate to the United States have come to realize that they must build up economical, financial, and social strength.

The Chinese help the Chinese and support their businesses; the Jews support the Jews, and even the Mexicans are supporting each other, to help one another get up on their feet.

It is very difficult for the black man to do this, for he has been taught to not trust each other, and to try to hold each other back. It is like the crap mentality-when you try to pull one crab out of the bucket, all the other crabs grab hold of it and hold it down.

But, we must break that mentality, and began investing in each other. No, mom and pop stores on the corner cannot compete with the retail, supermarket giant Walmart, but we should support them anyway, for they are our people. We might have to pay a couple of pennies or a dollar or so more, but we have got to lend out and help others in our ranks; and those that have been helped, but reach back and help somebody else come up and out.

White America did not include us, the black man, in the Declaration of Independence, and no, they did not include us in the original Constitution, and how could they, for many of them that signed the Constitution had slaves of their own.

We will lessen our disenfranchisement by strengthening ourselves, and investing in each other. We must build up our wealth and social status, and become strong politically; then, Mr. Charlie is forced to recon with us.

If we buy most of General Motors Cadillacs, then we can pool together and go to General Motors with some requests, no demands, and say we want this or that to happen within your company or else we shall stop supporting you; and because they love green more than they hate black, they will make the changes that request of their company.

We must stop driving the new car, but have nowhere to park it; stop buying the most expensive purse, but no money in the bank, and stop wearing the designer clothes and shoes, but no money in our pockets-broke with an expensive look.

Thus, the black man will enfranchise himself in this country, amongst his white constituents. We must stop waiting for a handout, or a hand up from those that don't have our best interest at heart. We must be the hand extended for us.

Enfranchisement and power starts with us, in our own home, and in our own communities.

We must stop waiting for some outsider to come and police our neighborhood.

We must go back to loving ourselves, and realizing that black is beautiful.

We must not stoop to the levels of hate; for hate is a poison that ultimately destroys he to whom bosom it rests in.

We must empower us-by us, for us.

Chapter Two

Our new old self

Mr. Charlie, in order to give himself an outlet, and justification, and to moralize his own evil horrific ways, he has to some way and somehow demonize those to which he lunges his undue contempt upon-whether it's the Indian, or Mexican, or Puerto Rican, or Jew, or the one that he has faithfully called Negro. The white man has to cleanse his own conscious by vilifying those that he so unjustly mistreat and use for his own self-fulfillment.

He must prove me, the black race, bad in order to show himself good; the black man has to be looked upon as evil in order for Mr. Charlie to become angelic-even amidst his wickedness. He cannot justify his actions towards the black race unless he dehumanizes them; else, he becomes demonic himself.

It is a paradox; for the white man's generations upon generations of hate and abuse towards the black man has left himself marred, corrupt and hollow. Though, he'll never admit it, he has painfully learned that putting someone else's light out doesn't make yours shine brighter; sometimes, it dims your light the more.

Mr. Charlie sits in his plush office of psychology, and ponders the black man; and under the pretense of bewilderment, he shakes his head as though he knows not why the black man thinks and acts as he does.

But, their own white men of higher education in the field of psychology, their doctors, ascribe that heredity plus environment, equals behavior.

Huh? That means that where he came from, and where he lives now, mixed together, produces his behavior now!

Mr. Charlie cannot just simply sit back and wash his hands of us now. No, all that I am, he made me; the burning anger nestled in my bosom, he helped to put there. Our disposition on things and acquiring more stuff to make us feel like somebody, he put in us.

He taught us to hate the man that we see in the mirror, to abhor the very color of our skin, the pigment that identifies us. Mr. Charlie taught me to hate myself and anybody that looked like me; so thus, the black man fries his hair with chemicals, and bleach the hell out of his skin, and even tries desperately to change the way that he talks-all in an futile attempt to "look" like Mr. Charlie, his oppressor. Why, so that he will be accepted and respected in this very white world that the white man thinks that he created for himself.

But, to the black man's dismay, he soon finds out that the white man does not care if you dye and fry your hair straight and make it blond like his; he doesn't care whether you bleach your skin pale to look like him, or wear color contacts in your eyes to turn them blue like his; he still hates you because you can never stop being YOU; confused, but still you -A black man that is desperately trying to be white.

Our willingness to fight friends and foes alike, and our willingness to flight rather that grab hold of our responsibilities all stem back to him-Mr. Charlie. For over four hundred years, he was our teacher, and yet still is; for even now, he is yet teaching us.

Do not think that one can keep a people in slavery for over four hundred years, and then set them free-not entirely free, and then expect them to recover and be alright in just a short time; sometimes, it will take another four hundred years for that people to fully recover from the sickening treatment of slavery.

And, Mr. Charlie and many of his constituents ponder why the black man acts like he does.

He discusses amongst his colleagues why does the black man always wants a hand-out from the government. Well, maybe it is not altogether a handout. Maybe it is still that deep burning yearning that the United States government still owes him something-forty acres of land, and a borrowed mule.

Immediately, after the civil war, the government, acting through their General-William Sherman had promised the former slaves of the south forty acres of land. They were to inhabit all of the land previously owned by the Union that fought the war against the United States government. The government had confiscated the land and gave it to the slaves for free.

This move was more of a strategy of post war than anything else; that is the reason why the ex-slaves never received the land. It was to give them something to dream for to keep them from going back to their previous slave owners.

There are two concise reasoning behind the land move: 1. So that the previous slaves wouldn't go back to just being slaves. 2. The Union soldiers wouldn't have any resources to replenish and start the fight afresh.

General Sherman's promise to them was that they would have the land of the previous Union soldiers for free, and that they would be a government unto themselves.

The gift of the forty acres never came to fruition, for President Lincoln's successor sympathized with the Southerners, and eight months later, he rescinded the order and gave the land back to the original owners-The Southerners.

So, yes, as descendants of the newly freed slaves and the promise of forty acres of land, we fill a sense of owing to us; a very real sense of entitlement.

The Civil War was fought from 1861 to May of 1865. After the civil war ended and the North declared victory, the United States added the Thirteenth Amendment, in December of 1865, to the Constitution which abolished slavery and freed all slaves.

Amidst the war, President Lincoln signed the emancipation proclamation executive order which declared that all slaves in the states that were fighting the Union states were freed, which freed over three million black people.

Many blacks celebrate this action as an honorable act of President Lincoln freeing the slaves, but this was simply a military maneuver; for it was done to weaken the south's fighting force.

The Union prevailed and conquered the South, and passed new laws to governed the new United States.

The problem with the newly passed laws was Washington's law makers, to somewhat appease the southern slave owners, they allowed the slave owners to gradually come in line with the law.

The other problem was that the slave master would go to his slaves and tell them that they were now free and that they could go wherever they wanted to.

They had no education, no vocation, and the only thing that most of them knew was slavery-working on Mr. Charlie's plantation; so when Mr. Charlie came and told them that they were now free, and that they could go wherever they wanted to, the majority of them chose to stay on the plantation. The new name for slavery was "Sharecropper".

You see, when the war ended, it didn't end racial prejudice; it didn't make the white man see the ex-slaves as equals. No, they lynched them even more than before because they were bitter about losing the war.

Congress realized that the South was not adhering to the new law of the Thirteenth Amendment added to the Constitution wherein it made slavery illegal and freed all slaves; so to strengthen the Thirteenth Amendment, on July of 1868, Congress passed the Fourteenth Amendment, which in essence, simply put, declared that all persons, born in the United States, United States citizens.

In 1865, the black slaves were set free by law, and then in 1868, they were made legal United States Citizens-seeing now, by now, all of the slaves were born into slavery in the United States.

And, even after becoming freed United States citizens, the new citizens were not allowed to vote, so the white man controlled the ballad box, which enabled him to put people in office that thought like he thought. Hence, the Jim Crow laws and segregation stood mightily in the South.

Then, Congress, in 1870, passed the Fifteenth Amendment to the Constitution; which gave all male citizens of the United States the right to vote.

So thus, in 1865 the slaves are freed; in 1868 the freed slave is made a United States citizen, and in 1870, he is given the right to vote.

Now, remember the Declaration of Independence and The Constitution of the United States-"We the People", and "All men are due certain rights." You understand now why I said that the black man was not included in the Declaration of Independence or the Constitution because if he was they would not have had to amend The Constitution.

Amend means to add to or change something. Thus, because the black race was not originally included in The Constitution, or thought of in The Declaration of Independence, he had to be amended in, and even then, it was a accepted to be a gradual change.

Slavery was not just a United States condition; it was all over the world-including Britain, Spain, Sweden, Netherlands, France, Portugal, Danish, West Indies, Brazil, the Caribbean, Cuba, and so on....etc....etc....etc. Most nations practiced slavery, even from the bible days; remember, Joseph brothers sold him as a slave to the Egyptians.

For most nations, slavery was a commodity, a very rich commodity. But, soon the nations began to outlaw slavery. Not because their conscious was pricked, but because the slave commodity began to lose value. It began to be more expensive to care for a group of slaves.

So they began to outlaw the act of slavery; starting as such:

Britain led the way in outlawing slavery in 1807.

Spain in 1811

Sweden in 1813

Netherlands in 1814

France in 1826

Portugal in 1819

Danish West Indies in 1846

Brazil in 1851

The Caribbean in 1861

The United States in 1865

And, lastly Cuba in 1886

In 1948, the United Nations wrote a universal declaration on Human rights, and decried that slavery and the slave trade shall be prohibited in all nations in all their forms-that included forced servitude as well.

So you see that the black man's fight for justice, liberty, and life was not just reserved to the United States of America; no, he struggled all over the world-even in his own country, black Africa-where he is the majority, and the white man is the minority.

Chapter Three

A black identity crisis

I Ain't Nobody's Negro

The Negro was developed and taught who and what he should be; he was in fact a piece of property whose identity was dependent upon somebody else, somebody with white skin that was consumed by white privilege.

What the white man understands conclusively, and always has, is that if one does not know who they are, then, they are more apt to become who someone else wants them to become.

From the time the black man entered the slave world until his dying day, he was systematically stripped of his identity-his name, his culture, his religion, his diet, his language…..etc…..etc…..etc.

When the African got off of the slave ship, even while riddled in fetters and chains, he was given a new European name, and culture. The African was systematically stripped of "self".

He was stripped of his self, and made into someone else, or to put it more accurately, made into someone's property. He was manipulated to hate his very black soul, and to see everything labeled black as bad, and everything labeled white as good and pure; thus, you have:

Black market-Where something is sold illegally.

Black balled-Someone that is shunned by others.

Black magic-Evil power

Black list-A list of troubled people, or unsuitable and un-usable

Black out-A time when a city or place has lost power and in the dark

Black Friday-A day when everything is cheapened

Blackened meat-Meat that is chard or burned

Even some of our foods are labeled to give this psychological perspective, such as, a devil's food cake is chocolate, and an angel food cake is white-perpetuating the image of black as bad, and white as good.

It is no wonder that the black man and woman have a difficult time relating or even discovering who they really are.

Black has been portrayed as so utterly bad to him, until the black man and woman will often times do whatever they can to their skin and hair to deviate from their black heritage.

Thus, is the reason why the black man and woman will fry their hair to make it straight and get rid of their natural kinky African hair texture; they would take a hot iron and pull it through their hair until it became silky straight like the white man, and they will dye their hair blond and put colorful eye contacts in their eyes-attempting to look as white as Mr. and Mrs. Charlie-the white man and woman.

They will use bleaching cream to bleach the black color from their skin because over and over the white world has taught the black man that black is bad.

And, what is utterly amazing about it all is it matters not how so ridiculous and funny they look, they still try to wear that white look.

I see it on the streets all the time-a very black woman wearing a blond wig or dying her hair blond or red, with blue contacts in her eyes; she looks mixed up, but in her psychological mind, she is beautiful because she is an image of the white woman she is trying to portray, or better still, her mentality is that she has become "the white" woman, and has abandon the blackness that she has been taught down through the years was ugly.

The white man enhances the black man's self denial even further through his religion. His picture of Jesus the Christ is with straight hair, white skin, and blue eyes-a white Jesus.

Any rational mind knows that Jesus could not have looked like that being born and raised in Israel, but the black man does not question it, he just accepts it, which furthers his desires to be white-like Jesus.

We never once considered how and why the white man even Europeanized Jesus twelve disciples. Note the names of the twelve disciples: Peter, James, John, Andrew, Thomas, Matthew, Phillip….etc.….etc.

It is quite difficult to even imagine an Israelite giving their children English names. A child's name was very important to the Israelites.

Too, when one travels through the entire bible, one finds mostly English names. I submit to you that this, no doubt, happen during King James scribes translation of the bible.

Our white brothers always has a propensity to want to make everything "white"-even the bible-right down to where it is recorded, "Slaves, obey your masters." Telling the slaves, through the scriptures, don't seek to be free.

Every time the bible is translated "for better understanding", some things are dropped from it while other things are added-through the years, man tampering translations has watered the bible down to fit his own way of living.

The thrust here, is to make what the black man worships appear to be white, thereby, continuing to foster that "white is good" image upon the black minds, both young and old. Their teaching is, "just obey".

You see, the greatest injustice of slavery is not that of the body, but that of the mind.

You can take the chains off of his ankles and wrist, but if you keep him with a slave mentality, then he becomes even more of a slave, and even more bound than before.

The slave becomes satisfied, and even proud of being Mr. Charlies' slave, for he identifies with the white man's color as that of pure and right, and just, and good; but black as something to abhor and change.

So, the black man has a very real identity crisis.

The black man, because he sees white as good and pure and beautiful, when he becomes truly successful, often times, one of the first things that a black man will do is go and date or marry him a white woman; she epitomizes his success.

He has been taught and brain washed over the years to see his own black women as not as beautiful as the white woman, so he launches out to ascertain the so called beautiful white woman-then, he feels truly successful.

I am not expostulating that there is something innately wrong with marrying or dating whites, but what is wrong is to do so simply because they are white.

My personal feelings are that one should stay within their own race, but that is just my personal feeling.

When I go home, I want to go home to someone that looks like me, and can relate to what I go through from day to day as a black man. I don't feel that a white woman can truly completely "feel" my day to day struggles. She has lived under white privilege all of her life, so how can she truly understand and embrace my struggles.

It is as it has been previously quoted; the whites telling us to pull ourselves up by our own bootstraps, and when we look down, we have neither boots nor straps.

This is the reason why I believe that integration hurt the black race more than it helped them; for when we became integrated and went to their schools and grasped completely and voluntarily grasped their culture and mannerism, our children took on their mannerism, and became disrespectful, and talked back to their parents and teachers because they saw the white children disrespecting their parents and talking word for word to the teachers, and all sorts of other disrespectful things at home, and this white attitude of the new integrated black youth even spilled over into the public arena, but they failed to realize that white America would not tolerate their disrespect as it did their white counter part.

And, not only did integration change our youth in the schools, but the effect of it migrated into our homes, and change the very fiber of black parenting.

Those first integrated black students grew up and became parents; thus, their parenting skills reflected that of the white parents. No, like the white parents, they didn't believe in getting a belt or switch and whipping the child like grandmama and granddaddy did to discipline them.

They began to believe like the white parents, that whippings were too cruel, so they just made them stand with their faces to a wall for a short time "time out".

This "time out" never worked because it led to the conduct of unruly children that the black parents could no longer control (even today-right now).

The child rules them, and they find themselves telling the child that if he doesn't act right and stop being bad, they are going to call his grandparents.

A child is not supposed to respect anyone more than he respects his own parents. The old mentality was, "No, I am not going to call grandma on you; I am going to tell grandma how I whipped your butt" and oftentimes, grandma would also whip the child for acting a fool on his parents.

Sunday mornings, during church, I often see young parents that cannot control their children. They cannot enjoy church service or hear what the preacher is telling them what God has said because their child is sitting in church unruly and out of control. They spend most of their time in church trying to appease the child.

I've witnessed where one of the parents would have to go sit in the lobby with the unruly child while the other parent tried to enjoy a little of church service, and then they would switch with each other.

Isn't it different! Before we adopted white parenting, all the black parent would have to do when the child began to act unruly during church service, was just look at him, and he would began to calm down and act right because he knew that there were consequences for his actions, and consequences that usually did not wait until he got home.

Even the Bible addresses the issue of how to handle unruly children. Note: Proverbs 23: 13-14:

13. Withhold not correction from the child: for if you beat him with the rod he shall not die.

14. You shall beat him with the rod, and shall deliver his soul from hell.

Proverbs 13: 24:

24. He that spares his rod hates his son: but he that loves him chastens him betimes.

The black home became a spitting image of the character of the white home, and the children and parents simply emulated the actions of the white folks' home.

Black youth which was now integrated into the white schools, perused their new white associate's life style, and gradually started immolating them to the point to where the black youth, just as his new found white associate, began acting with a sense of entitlement, and his behavior and speech became abrasive to the law and those that were in authority.

And, in the streets, our children are shot down like dogs because they think that they can be disrespectful and wild like the white kids, and speak their minds like the white kids, but fail to get away with it because, at the end of the day, our black babies are still our black babies, sometimes confused by their white friends, but still, non-the- less, our babies.

Our youth fail to realize that they can't expect to get the same fare treatment on the streets as their white counterpart for when a white man says how he feels, they say that he is just speaking his mind, but when a black man says what is on his mind, they label him as being militant and contrary.

White society will not let them forget that they "are not white", but still very much black, and has a different set of rules applied to them.

Because of the identity crisis amongst the few rich black athletes that make it to the big league, and put white women on their arms, our young men desires to be just like them and escort a white girl on their arm, because then he feels like the successful athlete-he is great because he has a white girl on his arm.

But, soon, the black man, like O.J. Simpson, is soon abruptly and brutally awakened to a real painful reality. It doesn't matter how rich you are, and how many white girls that you marry or date, you are still, to them, but a black man that happens to have a confused white woman by his side; that is what they think; and they feel and treat the white woman as less because she has chosen a black man; to them, it lessens her.

The white mindset and mentality has been so thoroughly shaped and brained washed until it matters not what the white man's plight is, or his economical status, or his education, he could be at the bottom of the barrel of life, and he will still think that he is better than the black man, even though, many times the black man is more educated, more economically sound, and has status amongst his peers. The white mind still sees him as less and not an equal.

So many black rich men suffer with the identity crises like O.J. Simpson. Often, when asked to help the black cause, O.J Simpson would respond that he was not black, but he was simply O.J. Simpson, but when troubles struck, he soon discovered that he was not just O.J. Simpson, the famous football player; he was a black man that had been accused of murdering a white woman. He had a rude awakening, but I don't think that, even now, he has fully and truly learned his lesson; for he still appears to levitate towards white women.

Too, White society perpetuates the black man's identity crisis in law enforcement, the justice system, and the prison system-all sends the coherent message that black is not good, but marred, corrupt, and ugly; that's the picture that the black man is shown on a day to day basis.

Just take a panoramic look at the United State prison system; how it psychologically paints a picture of the worth of black life in America.

The U.S has a population of over 323,000,000 people, and only about 13% of the population is black. The black man is definitely a minority in the United States, but yet he makes up more than half of the prisoners incarcerated in the U.S.

Note, there are over 4,575 prisons in operation spread out over the United States with 2.2 million inmates. There are more prisons and prisoners in the U.S than any other nation in the world, with China coming in at second with 1.5 million inmates. China's population is 1.379 billion.

Whites make up over 77% of the United States population, so if all things were equal, just from a numerical point of view, it would seem more that reasonable to assume whites to be the majority in the prisons because they outnumber substantially every other ethnic group in the states.

But, of course, that is not the case, and no one seems to be paying any attention to the numbers-no one that matters anyway.

If justice was truly blind, and see not color, then whites would outnumber every other ethnic group in prison merely because there is a vast difference in the number of them as opposed to the number of other ethnic groups living in the United States.

If it is not injustice, and has nothing to do with race, how else then can we explain the prison inmate numbers of a 13% minority outnumbering a 77% majority.

All of the environment delivers a strong identity crises upon the black race; so thus, when he looks in the mirror at himself, psychologically he has been taught not to like what he are she sees.

It is because of their failed identity that the black race goes out and buys cars and houses and jewelry, and designer clothes, and name brand shoes that they cannot afford. They are trying desperately to ascertain the prosperity image of white America.

Chasing the "image" of wealth and prosperity, like the white man, is the reason why a black woman will buy and carry an eight hundred dollar purse, and yet live in substandard housing, with an overflow of unpaid bills.

It is the reason why black mothers will go out and buy their young four year old children expensive Air Jordan shoes, or a hundred dollar Ipod, and buy their jobless teenagers several hundred dollar Iphones. Why? Because they want to project "the image" of the wealth that the white man projects-not fully understanding that the wealth that the white man has acquired, he stole, or took by force, or connived, or tricked somebody else out of, or illegally got altogether.

The identity crisis is the reason why the black man will go out and finance a seventy thousand dollar Mercedes Benz, and have no place to park it, or, their car cost more or just as much as their house; and, it is the reason why some of them will go to the furniture store and buy a ten thousand dollar bedroom suit to put in a rented apartment-it just doesn't make any sense at all except that he reasons that "stuff{" will make him equal to Mr. Charlie.

And too, white America knows how much importance that the black race places upon "things" and "stuff", so they are quick to loan them money for stuff, but won't loan them money for a home which is one avenue to generate some degree of equity for the family.

Yes, Mr. Charlie will loan the black man money to buy more stuff, but not a home; he will loan him money for a car, which depreciates as soon as it is driven off the lot, but won't loan him money to start a business that will produce generational wealth and respectability.

Many of the black families are house poor though because they often times buy a house that they really cannot afford because the house absorbs most of their income.

You see, what is astoundingly amazing about all of this is that this identity crisis has been amongst the black man ever since his slave status was lessened by the white man.

His thought process was in order to "be somebody" you had to be like Mr. Charlie, and Mr. Charlie lived in the big white plantation house with a piano in it.

When Booker T. Washington came to the south to start a school to help the black man's mind, and elevate him to higher levels, he realized how deep rooted slavery was imbedded in them, but he was determined to elevate their minds-because one will never experience real change without a real paradigm shift.

The black ex-slave often acquired stuff that he didn't need, and sometimes, didn't even really want, but they did all of this to project an image that psychologically says that he is just as Mr. Charlie.

Booker T. Washington said that every other Negro shack that he visited had a piano in it; even though nobody in the house could play the piano, and even though most of them didn't even have a spoon or fork in the shack to eat with, they ate from their plates with their hands; still they had a piano because that meant status to them-like the white man.

When Booker T. Washington came to the south, he was simply flabbergasted. He just couldn't believe their thought process, and how much they value things of little worth simply because the white man had them, or the white man did it.

They do all of this to project an image that psychologically says that he is just as Mr. Charlie.

Hence, he becomes a different kind of slave, but still but a slave, and, through this mental method, he teaches his children to be a new kind of slave; for when he dies, he has no wealth to pass on to his children, only bills; so the failed identify trend perpetuates itself into the next new generation; never really accepting and appreciating the beauty of who they are and building there upon.

The black man has been taught and trained, often times subliminally, and psychologically, to immolate and duplicate the white man; so, though he, himself is black, he has been taught overtly and subconsciously to be as "whitish" as he can be, even to the point of hating his own beautiful, and very black skin.

The black man never seems to pause and look around himself, and ponder if he is not beautiful, then why else would so many Caucasians lie all day in the sun, and risk skin cancer, trying to darken their skin as the black man; or why do they spend millions of dollars each year on tanning salons trying to darken their skin-it is because black is inherently beautiful!

But, one's self worth can only be acquired and appreciated from within; it matters little how much worth the outside considers you, if you cannot value and see your own self worth; thus is the paradox piercing the hearts of the black man and woman.

The black man's identity crisis is pushed upon him even from a child, for when the black mother and black father go to the store to buy a doll for their little girl to play with, they purchase a white baby doll; at Christmas time, the black man has been taught from a child that a white man is going to come to his house on Christmas eve and leave some toys for him. Mind you, the black parent is the one that has labored and spent their earning to buy toys and gifts for their children, but they tell the children that Mr. Charlie, the white man, in a red suit, came and brought them the gifts while they slept.

How preposterous is that? A white man, driving a magical slay, is going to come in our Hood at midnight, with a bunch of expensive gifts, and leave them at our house while we sleep.

The psychological picture that that paints is that daddy and mama didn't give their children anything, but the white man in the red suit did, thereby diverting the child's thanks from the black parent to the white man. So, instead of the child thanking his parents, he thanks the white man for being so generous to him.

And, that is the same lie that their mama and daddy taught them, so when the child grows up, they too, will teach their children of how generous the white man is, and they will teach their children, and the next generation will teach their children, so the identity crisis is perpetuated from generation to generation.

Seemingly, logic would grasp the parent to teach their babies the truth, so that they will be thanking daddy and mama for their sacrificial gifts that they gave to their children, rather than thanking someone that had virtually nothing to do with it.

The task of wiping away the identity crisis amongst black people is laid heavily upon the parents; for the child will not know unless the parents teach them.

The importance of this point of parental teaching is illustrated in the Bible when God instructed Moses to tell the children of Israel to teach their children. Note: Deuteronomy 11: 18-19:

18. Therefore shall you lay up these my words in your heart and in your soul, and bind them for a sign upon your hand, that they may be as frontlets between your eyes.

19. And you shall teach them your children, speaking of them when you sit in your house, and when you walk by the way, when you lie down, and when you rise up.

Note what God says of Abraham concerning the importance of teaching his children of who they are: Genesis 18: 18-19

18. Seeing that Abraham shall surely become a great and mighty nation, and all the nations of the earth shall be blessed in him?

19. For I know him, that he will command his children and his household after him, and they shall keep the way of the Lord, to do justice and judgment; that the Lord may bring upon Abraham that which he has spoken of him.

Observe what Joshua says to the congregation concerning teaching their children: Joshua 4: 5-7:

5. And Joshua said unto them, Pass over before the ark of the Lord your God into the midst of Jordan, and take you up every man of you a stone upon his shoulder, according unto the number of the tribes of the children of Israel;

6. That this may be a sign among you, that when your children ask their fathers in time to come, saying, What mean you by these stones?

7. Then you shall answer them, That the waters of Jordan were cut off before the ark of the covenant of the Lord; when it passed over Jordan, the waters of Jordan were cut off: and these stones shall be for a memorial unto the children of Israel for ever.

So, you can clearly see the importance that God places upon the parent teaching and unveiling their past unto them so that they will always be reminded of "who" they are.

The black race falters in their identity because generation after generation was taught by the white man of who they are.

If we do not teach each succeeding generation who they are, then somebody else, the white society, will; for someone else is always willing and ready to tell you who you are.

And, if they can tell you who you are right now, then, they systematically wipe away, or hide very deeply, who you were and who you really are in this present moment.

They further still the black man's knowledge of his true identity by the infiltration of drugs into our neighborhoods.

But they say that we cannot blame the white man for drugs in our neighborhoods; I sternly protest and confess emphatically that yes we can, for all the drugs start somewhere in white hands.

No, they don't come directly to our communities. The real dealers are uptown living in penthouses or on the lavish other side of town sending dope into our communities by his black flunky.

Most of the drugs, particularly the hard drugs, come to the United States from overseas. And, most of my people do not own ships or planes; no, the white man brings it in and then distributes it to our people-destroying our neighborhoods and further sabotaging the identity of the black race.

I found it most strange though, that when drugs were invading the black community, they labored us as dope addicts, and users that needed to be put away in prison somewhere; and then, when drugs started invaded the white community and the young white boys, and well to do upscale white collar workers became users, they labor it now as "a disease" and the users are simply sick and need help.

Drugs are on all of our street corners surrendering our babies, young men, young women, and even elders. It is an epidemic pervading the black race.

But, of all the things that I have here-to-fore written of that has stolen or helped to hide the black man's true identity is **RELIGION!!!!**

It has been said that when the white slave owners, on their big plantations with many slaves, would have problems with an uprising or unhappy slave group, he would tell his slaves to go to church and have several nightly meetings of church because Mr. Charlie knew that that would calm the slaves down, and soon, they would go back to the fields laboring the same horrendous labors, but feeling better because of the church meeting that they had come out of days before.

So, even now, they still use religion to sooth the black man and help him remain content in the racial, discriminative, unjust, state that he resides in.

Just turn on your television to the religious channels, and you will find that 99% of them (both black and white) are talking about "get more" and "have more". They bellow from the pulpit, "Get your blessings right now, and your blessings are on the way."

Most preach little about righteous living, Godly living, but about riches achieved.

So, thus, Mr. Charlie coerce the black church going, God fearing, Christians to start believing that God is just their errand boy, to give them what they want, when they want it.

You hear them echoing to the poor and struggling, "Send me your money and I'll send you some of my oil or holy clothes that will make blessings and money and health come to you."

Is it not crazy! Jesus said that whatever gifts that you have, freely God gave it to you, so freely you should assist others with it.

I suspect that I should pause and say parenthetically that I am not expostulating giving to the cause of the church to help further the gospel, and help the poor. No, I just think that we lose who we are when we try to make our God our pimp of an errand boy.

You see, the white preacher knows that the black man and woman are caught up in "stuff", because white America has taught them that "stuff" defines who you are, so he capitalizes upon their greed.

And, it is not just the white preachers; many of the black preachers are now immolating the reverend Mr. Charlie.

Many of the black preachers now sees how he can suck wealth from his parishioners and his T.V audiences; so, he too, like his white constituent declares to the poor struggling mom and dad who's looking for a way out, or looking for some degree of relief from their daily heart breaking struggles, that if they send him some money, often times their meager last, he will send them a blessing.

They struggle with their raggedy cars that they can't afford to repair because they have sent their last to the televangelist so that he can sport his lavish life style.

The black man has become so lost in his identity until whatever the white church does, he does also.

Rev. Mr. Charlie started having one church with several locations, then, low and behold, yes, you guessed it; some black preachers started having one church with multiple locations.

On a personal note, I just think that it is simply ludicrous to go to church to see a man preach on a screen when one passes by a multitude of churches with pastors that you can go to where one can physically see the preacher; physically touch him, and physically be counseled by him. The church was not designed to contain Gospel super stars reeling their position and status over the less fortunate.

All of it is simply confusing the few blacks because as we exit our black churches, we leave behind our roots of who we really are, and the black church struggles because they take their money, time, and resources to the white congregation, or the mega churches because that represents status.

While I must too pause and assert right here that "we" both blacks and whites should be one church with a multiplicity of ethnicities amongst us, but reality dictates that that is not the case.

The church is the most segregated place in America, and Sunday mornings are the most segregated times of the week.

White churches are still white churches with a few token black members which are usually confused thinking that they are better now because they go to church with the white folks-I am just stating a fact as I see it to be.

Black churches are still black churches with a few token white folks that like the flavor and spice of black people worship.

The buildings don't make us; who we are is instilled in our hearts, which is the reason why the government will never be able to force us to have good relationships with each other, because one cannot legislate love.; it is a matter of a regenerated heart.

They've become the legendary Robin Hood, but unlike the legendary Robin Hood that stole from the rich to give to the poor, they still from the poor to fatten their own bank account.

The poor television parishioners pay for their mansions, their jets, and their Rolls- Royce.

And, all of these, greedy gain seeking preachers are helping to further the identity crisis amongst the black congregants, not realizing that "things" will never produce the royalty in them.

King Solomon alluded to this in his writings. He said, "A fool and his money will soon part."

It is very difficult and almost impossible to bring the king and queen out of a people if they never ever realize or see themselves as kings and queens, or the offspring of a great people.

No, we cannot all be great, or famous, or super rich, or royal, but it is imperative that we know who we are, then it is easier to become who I was meant to be, and easier for me to walk in my destiny, or change what has been forced upon me, to become what I choose to be-Black and Proud!!

Chapter Four

Black Attitude- Snap and Pop

White America oftentimes looks at us in amazement and shakes their heads at black people because of their disposition and flavorful attitude.

But, if one was to research the original black African, one would find a people that are rich and filled with spicy attitude and high expression.

Too, the white man played a significant role in today's African American's attitudes and disposition. He cannot separate himself. Mr. Charlie must accept being the central culprit laying the flippant, spicy disposition upon the black man.

Even a dog, if you continue to hit him every time that he sees you, will begin to run and react whenever he sees you. So it is with the black race; along with our innate culture and heritage, the white man fostered a disposition in the black man that he cannot soon shake off.

How can you expect anyone to continue to be kind and mild mannered when they are constantly mistreated-even while supposedly free?

Note some of the inherent things that gave the black people that popping, snapping disposition:

The white man would slaughter their hogs and take all of the meat that he thought was eatable, and leave the rest for the underprivileged black people. He would leave the hog's feet, tail, head, ears, intestines, and whatever else that he thought was despicable and of no use.

But, what he failed to realized was that the black people were resilient in their efforts to survive; so they took that meat of the hog that Mr. Charlie had given to them, because he thought that it was no good, and put herbs and spices in it, and made the no good meat taste good.

Then, Mr. Charlie started asking the black women that cooked for him to start preparing his food as such.

But, still, this was one of the things that built up that whip snap disposition in the black men and women-particularly the women.

All of this built up an attitude in the black disposition. It, along with a host of other deplorable actions of the white man, burned an unquenchable anger in the black ex-slaves, and their children and future generations to come.

So, marvel not when our sisters roll her neck and pop her head while snapping her finger, it's an attitude from long ago.

Too, that ill treatment forced upon the black man, is the reason why he is often aggressive and outspoken. How else is he expected to act when he and his brothers are constantly profiled by the police who represent the white establishment and white privilege.

He is stopped because he is black; he is searched and arrested without probable cause because he is black, and he is gunned down without legal or moral repercussion because he is black, so marvel not that he has a popping disposition-it is the least that white America should expect.

Some liberals will quickly say that we can't blame the white man now for our ill fate in our neighborhoods and in our communities, but I beg to differ. Yes, we can!

Surely, if one has been molded and sculptured into something or anything for over four hundred years, then it would seem logical that it would perhaps take as much time to reestablish the offspring of the slaves.

But, because he had forgotten his language, his culture, his heritage, his nation, and his people, he was prone to become as his captors, and relish in his own inability to break the psychological chains of yester years filled with the horrors of slavery.

Observe the black woman's Eurocentric attitude that she has adopted from her white counterpart.

Like her white females, her attitude is she thinks that showing as much skin as possible when she dresses is sexy and appealing,

She has been coached to show much of her breast, and as much thighs and legs as she can, even to her panties line, and show as much of her butt with as tight and as short a skirt and jeans as she can.

This has become her attitude in dress; her white sisters have trained her to dress to leave the man little to imagine, and so she does.

Her abrasive attitude that she acquired from the white woman is, "I'll show you everything, but I am still a dignified lady."

Failing to understand that most black men are not going to carry a lady home to meet his mama like that; that is a recipe for disaster, and just parenthetically speaking, there oft to be some things left just for that special man's eyes only.

But, her European sisters taught her to dress full of attitude-show the man everything, and then dare him to be ungentlemanly about it.

I say to the sister, lower your hem line, and cover your breast, and loosen your jeans, if you want to be respected for who you are, and if you want a man to notice your intellect. He'll never notice the color of your eyes if you're slanging breast and thighs everywhere.

Yes, some of our sisters are well endowed with mama's inherited hips, and breast, but still demand to be respected for your mind, and save your body and its secrets for your husband-there oft to be some of a woman's sensual peeks and curves for her man's eyes only!

Sometimes, all that black folk had was attitude; we came from Africa with a lot of spicy attitude; that's the reason why one of the first things that the white slave owner would do to the newly acquired slave is try and break his attitude; for a broken man or woman is much more easier to control than one with attitude.

Down through the years one can always find where Mr. Charlie has always tried to change the attitude of the black man, for he knows all too well that your attitude often determines your altitude in life-how you act and react to things in life, will often determine how far or how high that you go in life.

Even in religion, black people have always had a close walk and relationship with their God- A strong belief that He will come and deliver them from their adversaries-the white man.

Sometimes, all that they had was their attitude in worshipping God!

On Sundays, they would put on their best- Their Sunday suit, Sunday dress, Sunday hat, and Sunday shoes; often times, these were the only dress up clothes that they had. It gave them an attitude of pride.

Their worship services were often long and highly charged and full of Holy Ghost filling emotions. Church was their place of refuge from many of the toils and misgivings of their lives. Church life help them to release some of the built up anger and tension acquired during their daily life of disparity and injustice.

In mid-summer, as hot as it could be, they would still dress up in their Sunday's best and go to church (that had no air conditioners), sweating everywhere, but it gave them an attitude of pride, for that was something that the white man couldn't take from them; though he tried his very best to pollute it.

But, down through the years, the black man mixing with the white man filtered also into his church life and relationship with God and worship.

The white man taught him that you can go to church on Sunday morning, and then go out at night and burn somebody's house down while you lynched a few others, while wearing your white sheets with a cross plastered on the front of them; and I might pause and add right here that they no longer wear their white robes with a cross plastered on it. Now they wear suits and ties with a gold cross dangling around their necks- the same people, they just dress differently to blend in better. They use the pen instead of the rope, and the law to perpetuate injustice and white privilege.

Yes, Mr. Charlie gave them an attitude of a watered down powerless, accept all, do all and nothing religion- A religion that gave them a good time on Sundays, but had no power through the week.

The black man had to learn the true Christ for himself; and learn the delivering power, and forgiving power, and the power to love even your enemies and those that are yet mistreating you while carrying a bosom filled with pain and emotional hurt.

Religion has always been used by the white man to help surrender the black man to an obeying servant to the white race.

The real Jesus had dark skin and brown eyes, that is why in scripture God sent Him to Egypt, and thus said, "Out of Egypt have I called my son."

Just think realistically for a moment; one cannot grow up under the hot baking sun of Israel and still have white or pale skin. It is just impossible.

Jesus blend in with the Nubian black people of Egypt because of his dark skin-He was a dark complexion man of Israel.

But, to get the black people to submit more readily to the white man, they changed the color of Jesus in earlier portraits from dark skin to white.

They painted a Caucasian Jesus; why, so that when the slave or freed black man looked at a picture of The Savior, Jesus Christ, they saw an image that looked like the white man that was enslaving them, and causing them great hardship, but they, often times, endured the mistreatment because the slave master resembled their God; thus, psychologically infusing them with a representation of an unjust, prejudice Jesus.

So, psychologically, the slaves rations that they must submit because their perpetrators are an image of The Son of God-their ill treatment comes from an Image of The Almighty. Physically, they submitted because psychologically they had been wounded right down to their very soul.

Also, in 1604 King James had appointed at least sixty scholars to translate the bible from the Bishops Bible, or the Geneva Bible into the more "understandable" bible-The King James version of the Bible. All had been translated down through the years from the original text-the Hebrew Bible, written in Hebrew/Aramaic.

In translating the Bible though, they could not easily dismiss their own political, social, and partisan interests.

The translators that supported the slave trade and conditions, helped their cause when they translated the bible. Note:

Ephesians 6: 5-9:

5. Servants, be obedient to them that are your masters according to the flesh, with fear and trembling, in singleness of your heart, as unto Christ.

6. Not with eye-service, as men pleasers; but as the servants of Christ, doing the will of God from the heart;

7. With good will doing service, as to the Lord, and not to men:

8. Knowing that whatsoever good thing any man does, the same shall he receive of the Lord, whether he be bond or free.

9. And, you masters, do the same things unto them, forbearing threatening: knowing that your Master also is in heaven; neither is there respect of persons with him.

Observe what the book of 1 Peter says of the slave matter: 1 Peter 2: 18-19:

18. Servants, be subject to your masters with all fear; not only to the good and gentle, but also to the forward.

19. For this is thankworthy, if a man for conscience toward God endure grief, suffering wrongfully.

They inserted these scriptures about the slaves being obedient as Godly so to help keep the slaves from revolting and obeying-thinking that it is the will of God.

So the snap popping attitude is deeply incrusted in the black race because of the gross injustice and physical and psychological degrading exerts down through history. Sometimes, all that the black man possess is his popping defiant attitude that says to the racist that he cannot completely diverge him from his God given path.

Mr. Charlie has always used religion to a great degree to control the black communities.

Just recently I had a very large Caucasian church (of course they have a few token black members) to contact me – It wasn't the pastor, but one of his assistant pastors. He sent me a message saying that The Church wanted to come and help us; so I replied, "help us how", and they said that they would come into the community and help mow seniors grass and help repair some houses.

Mind you, I am already told that they are doing a lot of wonderful things around Birmingham and its suburbs-which is seemingly good.

My reply back to them was, "I don't need you all to help us mow grass, or repair a few houses, If you want to help us, we want to start a school at our church to help elevate the minds of our youth."

I never heard from them again.

History has taught me to be cautious of the white man's extended hand of voluntary assistance.

The white man never does anything for nothing; he always has an underlying self-serving motive.

You see, there-in lies my concern with the supposed civil rights organization-The NAACP-National Association for the Advancement of Colored People.

It was formed by a white person, Miss. Mary White Ovington, and if it was created by a white person, I just tend to believe that, at the end of the day, it is essentially for the white people under the guise of helping black people out of black suffering-they excel their own, sometimes hidden agenda.

Although it is commonly reported that W.E. Dubois founded the NAACP, that is not at all correct.

Mary White Ovington was the founder of the NAACP, along with Morefield Storey (first president), Joel Springam (2nd president), and John Dewey which also cofounded ACLU-American Civil Liberties Union. All were white people.

What you had at the inception of the NAACP was a few white people that were full of socialism and imperialism whose cause were veiled by the injustices of the black people that they referred to as Colored People.

When one surmises it all, it is best explained by that old adage: The enemy of my enemy is my friend.

This is parallel to the interpretation of Abraham Lincoln's speech, when he quoted Jesus statement about a house divided can't stand. Abraham Lincoln wasn't talking about white folks and black folks; no, he was talking about white folks of the north and white folks of the south.

The slaves were simply a bartering piece thrown amidst it all-a bartering piece of commodity that was swiftly declining worldwide.

Too, I guess that it is still quite admirable that a few white folks would try to wrestle with the culprits of injustice to the black race, even if they did have their own veiled agenda.

Many Caucasians have always possessed this deep sense of responsibility for the black race; that somehow they automatically know what's best for us as a black race; and I guess that this thought process is instilled and perpetuated in them through America's sense of white privilege which leads to white pride that produces white arrogance. Arrogant enough to think that one is better than someone else simply because of the color of one's skin.

So, thus, is the reason why I was most apprehensive when the popular white church sought to volunteer to help the black community. It is the underlying motive that alarms me- The motive that is often overlooked and not seen.

Still, I often wonder why I never did hear back from them to assist us in forming a school to elevate the minds of our youth, but then, I guess it is explained by their common business practice towards black people: they will loan us money to buy a new car, but not money to buy a house, or loan us money to buy a house, but never money to start a business.

The white folks quickly ask why do black people have such bad attitudes, and so much fight in them.

Well, I guess it is best explained that this is a disposition that we acquired down through the years; an attitude that was both learned and inherited.

The psychologist teaches that heredity plus environment equals behavior. In other words, simplified, ones behavior is the end result of what one has gone through, and what one is going through right now.

Do you want to change our popping attitudes? Stop profiling us; do you want to change our attitudes? Give us the rights that are do all Americans; you want to change our attitudes? Afford us equal opportunity to a piece of the American dream.

Why do black folk have such a popping attitudes?

In our neighborhoods that are usually one hundred percent black, with a few tokens here and there, the convenience stores amongst us are usually owned by other ethnicities-Indians, Pakistanis, Chinese, Koreans, Whites; everybody except somebody behind the counter that looks like us. And, to add insult to injury, many of them have the audacity to attempt to treat their mostly black patrons with disrespect-they want my money, but they try desperately, when discharging me change, not to touch my hand; as though something is going to rub off on them.

Yes, we got attitudes, hot attitudes!!

The police (not all of them, I might say) that we were taught is supposed to serve and protect all of our citizens, more than often, protect the whites and abuse the blacks.

The white man does not have to be afraid of being pulled over by the police because he knows that he is going to be treated respectfully, but on the other hand, the black motorist that is pulled over by the police has cause for alarm because he is treated with great disrespect and harm.

The black man is not over reacting when he is nervous of being pulled over by the policemen because he knows that he can very easily be shot or jailed on a whim, and absolutely nothing be done to the perpetrator.

Some will quickly say that the situation between the blacks and the Police is getting worst.

It's not getting worst; police brutality has always occurred, the only difference now is that because of social media, the internet, facebook, and phone cameras, it is recorded and reported while the injustice is occurring, or immediately after it occurs.

It is cause for an attitude when you see a black man being shot down like an animal by the police, and then the police go to court and is found innocent.

We experience injustice over and over again, so wonder not why our attitudes are as such, but wonder at the amazement of how we have endured for so long, and kept a degree of sanity and respect.

Over all, black folk are law abiding people, and we want what every other American want-freedom, justice, the ability to care for our families, and to see our children given the opportunity to prosper just as any other.

We want our families to be safe and live in safe neighborhoods.

One of the things that gives us popping attitudes is when white America's courts and the law enforcements lump all blacks together, and charge all of us for the deeds of a few of us.

Many times, in some of the black neighborhoods, when the police come into the community, they have on their body armor; they are escorted by a swat team, and have dogs, and shot guns, and M16s, and they are adorned with helmets on their heads- All because they say that they are about to apprehend a dangerous criminal.

They often times do this when the perpetrator's crimes has invaded the white community or white man's business uptown or across town.

They fail to realize that we are just as afraid of those criminals as they are-fear is why they come so prepared.

But, we don't have a swat team to protect us; we don't have body armor, or M16s; still, we are afraid just as they are, and because we often don't get protection, we develop attitudes because we are unsafe and it appears that the courts, the government, and law enforcement don't care.

The younger generations of blacks, generation X, generation Y, generation Z, and the Millennial generation, are not as patients as their forefathers- the baby boomers, that patiently and prayerfully endured and sometimes accepted the discrimination and racial inequality actions of some of their misguided white Americans.

They have tasted the freedom and equality of their white associates. Integration exposed to them the privileged white world, and they, rightly so, want the same rights, and they are not willing to wait because wait, to the black man, means never.

Having been constantly denied our rights as American citizens, and human rights as God's children, sometime all that the black man has is a popping attitude. It has become part of the way that he survives the injustice and brutality of the life of a black man living in his home place of America.

He is constantly under stress and tension.

The black man faces racial tension and discrimination constantly in this land that is defined as freedom for all-the melting pot of the world.

He just wants to be given the same respect, rights, and privileges that are given to the Caucasians.

The black man is tense and sometimes fearful because he has learned all too well that injustice is everywhere that he turns; he can't get away from it; his education won't deliver him from it; having a better job doesn't deliver him from it. Living in a nicer neighborhood doesn't deliver him from it, so he is constantly ravaged by injustice-and because so often, they have taken everything else from him; all that he has left is a popping attitude that is full of fight; ready to fight somebody, everybody, and anybody-it has been bottled up, and now, he is always on the verge of exploding.

The black race possess an attitude filled with an explosive energy that he cannot fully explain; he only knows that it is there amidst brokenness, hurt, shame, and unfulfilled dreams and abandoned hope for a better tomorrow because every day living in his world has taught him that tomorrow mean more of the same of what has already been.

Chapter Five

The Black Queen

Dear Mama

I've never stopped to show you how much I love you
And appreciate all the wonderful things that you do
Most men have not even a clue
How you hold the family together like motherly glue

I've watched you be strong when I knew you should have been weak
Your reward, your child's happiness is all you seek
In the midst of the storm when all seemed bleak
you without hesitation denied yourself so your child could eat

To nurture me, sometimes you took food off your plate to put on mine
And when I refuse to obey, you put more than a scolding on my behind
You stressed stay in school and develop your mind
For in the streets there is nothing good to find
So you made me be home by nine
You taught me to never ever to any be unkind
And never cross the legal line

I watched you weep
When you thought that I was asleep
Because my daddy refused to help you raise me
So all on you I was left to be
A woman teaching a boy how to see

Dr. Akeam Amoniphis Simmons

The world full of opportunity
And endless possibility

I often wondered where your strength came from
But certainly hoped that I have some

I hope to make you proud of me someday
So you will know that it was not vain to raise me that way

Thanks mama for wiping away my tormented frown
And picking me up when I was knocked down

Thanks mama for not toilet flushing me
Even before I had eyes to see
Thanks mama for not allowing some doctor to abort me
And not even considering what it would cost to raise me

Without you there would be no me
Like man without the three
The Father, Son, and Holy Spirit-The trinity
Thanks mama for being my mama
Because of you, my children will know how to handle life's drama

The black woman, our black queen, the mother of us all, operates with a bosom full of tears and heartbreak; for while on the outside she displays immense strength and fortitude. She is ready to fight for her family, but on the inside, she is broken, bruised and battling depression.

She battles her own private depression, for she must remain strong for the rest of her clan. They absorb strength from her; that's why she scrubbed white folk's floors, and iron their clothes, and raised their children while cooking their meal without sometimes a mumbling word. She knew her family depended on her. And, most of the time, she labored all by herself without the assistance of a husband-she had to be both mama and daddy.

She often times came together with the other black females in her little village; they greatly depended on each other to help one another make it through, so they would help with their sister's children, cooking, and even house choirs-that's where we get the old saying that it takes a whole village to raise one child. She was not alone; she could count on the rest of her sisters, for all of them went through the same things.

The single most prevalent reason why the black race survived, and is yet surviving, and I would venture more deeply and say, even thriving, is because of the tenacity of the black women. She is the epitome of strength amongst her people.

The black woman, the queen amongst all women, she is our mother, our wife, our sister. She is the strength that keeps the black race afloat-the one that desperately tries to take away the conundrums amongst her people. She was Samson's hair; Solomon's wisdom, David's force, Adam's Eve, Gideon's sword, and Abraham's strength. She is the best of us; the gift amongst us that God gave unto us that just keeps on giving and refuse to be denied or defeated. The black Queen has brought back a nation of people who were even at the brink of death.

She is the one that gives the black race the resolve to keep fighting, keep developing, and keep moving higher. She refused to quit. And, I guess she really didn't have much of a choice if she wanted her race to continue moving forward.

Perhaps none amongst the black race has suffered more than she has; for she was forced to birth both black and white babies-raped often times by Mr. Charlie, and the appointed plantation black stud, while at the very same time birthing children for her own slave husband-all were the white man's property that he did with as he pleased.

They called her the Negro woman, which meant that she was strong and belonged to some white man. She could work in the fields, clean the house, and cook dinner, both for the white family and her own; many times, taking the left-overs from the plantation owners dinner to help feed her own family that had very little. After working for Mr. and Mrs. Charlie all day, she went home and labored, cooking, cleaning, teaching in her own house for her own family, and when the next day came, it came only for her to do it all over again and again.

Often times, the black family is only lead by mama because the black husband and father chose to walk away, but the black woman, mama, had no such luxury; love would not allow her to walk away and do better for herself; no, she had to stay and raise her babies by herself as best she could.

She bares the reason, not because she want to, why black folks range in so many shades of color; some even looking out right white, or as they said back then, many could pass for white.

The black woman held her and her children together as best she could, and for as long as she could-Most of the time the white slave master would force the Negro men, on the plantation, to "breed" with other strong Negro women (because they were, like all the other animals that he owned, his property).

Mr. Charlie took care of the children; he fed them, clothed them, sheltered them, and protected them because they were his property and future workers in whatever capacity that he chose for them.

The Negro man would often times gather under some tree when they had a break, and boast about how many children that he had, and which one of them had the most children, but none took care of their children-that was the white plantation owner's job.

Sounds familiar? Now you can understand now why many black men, right now, have a hands-off attitude towards their children. The black woman, now, just as the Negro woman then, has to struggle by herself and ask Mr. Charlie for assistance in raising her babies.

The only difference is now the white slave master has another name; he is called welfare, housing projects, food stamps etc......etc......etc. All from the white man to help the black woman, just as the Negro woman, take care of her babies while the black man, still having a Negro mindset, is running about pursuing his own dreams or just loathing through life; and sometimes, he too waits for Mr. Charlie's handouts.

Thus, it becomes a generational curse; the succeeding generation simply immolates the preceding generation.

It is the reason why we have such a large collection, in our neighborhoods, of Mama's boys; he refuse to work, and oftentimes looks for a woman with a good job to take care of him.

The black woman-the African American queen, has to struggle any way that she can to bring her children out of the substandard living, and the psychological ghetto placed upon them by white America through overt and subliminal messages-trying to steal and continue to enslave them if only through the pen partisan legislature

I shudder to even imagine where would we be without our Big ma and Madeas laboring with their sons, daughters, grandsons, and granddaughters. Even when she was just a Negro slave (white property), she prevailed.

When most of the male Negro slaves were afraid to revolt, for the white man had beaten the warrior spirit of Africa out of them, the female Negro slave refused to give up, even at the risk of their own lives and their children because if Mr. Charlie, the plantation owner, ever found out, he would kill her and her children, or whip them half to death. But, she was not deterred. She still revolted and resisted-though the men got the credit.

The Negro woman was a inherent fighter, which in turn, made her a fighting black woman. She constantly has to fight-for her children, her household, her liberty, and even for her man. As previously stated, many black men, when they become successful, run to a white woman, and the white woman is all too ready to strip him of his wealth, which in turn, strips his children and grandchildren of generational wealth.

They ask why does the black woman has an attitude; it is one of the things that keeps her going, for she never considered the choice to leave and walk out on her children that often times only had her.

She saved the Negro race before they became free and black. She had to be mama and daddy in the house, and while it is very difficult for a woman to teach a boy how to be a man, she did the best that she could.

The black woman works all day, sometimes two jobs, to take care of Children that she didn't bring here by herself, but she is by herself; laboring under the load of single parenting.

She stands in long lines, enduring the insults and preconceived prejudice, trying to get food stamps and welfare to help feed her babies.

And, through all of this, she is further insulted when the father of her children won't lift a hand to help her, but will assist another woman in rearing children that is not his.

The child that the black mother is struggling to raise only sees his daddy from afar, and often times, don't even know him until he is in his teens or grown. So it was with me, I first got to know who my father was when I was about eight years old, and met him when I was about twelve years old, and then, it was because I sought him out.

Mama labored with me and raised me the best that she could with the help of my grandmother and aunties. Yes, all were very strong black females;

not because they wanted to be, but because they had to be if their sons and daughters, like me, were going to survive.

I listen to some of these rappers talking about how "hard" they are, and how much of a gangster they are, while they show off their gold chains, diamond rings, and expensive cars; so many of our young men want to be like them, and associate themselves as rappers, so they won't work because "they say" that they are working on their music, and what little money they do get, they go and buy some glitter to cast that image that they see the rappers on T.V cast, but it is at the expensive of their babies.

Yes, it is alright to have a dream, but not at the expense of your son or daughter; that is too expensive, for it affects several generations.

Sometimes, a man's dreams has to be put on hold, while he helps his son become a man, and shows his daughters what a real man is, and what to look for when choosing a man.

It takes a real man to get under a thirty year mortgage, so that his family will have a place of their own; it takes a real man to get up every day and go to work, sometimes even to a job that he doesn't like so that he can put food on the table and clothes on his family's back; it takes a real man to get up on Sunday mornings and lead his family to church even when he is still tired from working all week, or maybe he has to go to work Sunday night. And, it takes a real man to go out and get two jobs because one doesn't adequately takes care of his family, and he'd rather work two than force his wife to have to.

Yes, being a real man is most difficult, which is the reason why most of the black homes are single parent homes led by mamas and grandmamas.

James Brown once wrote a song that said that this is a man's world, but it would be nothing without a woman or a girl- how profound, for she is the essence of our being-the seed from whence we grow. The deep depression in our stomachs (our navels) constantly reminds us that we were once completely connected to her mothers.

Yes, the black woman is strong because she has to be; most of the time, she has no choice; for her babies only has her to count on.

And, though she does all of this, she was not meant to; for even nature gives us subtle hints of who she was designed to be. Her shoulders are narrow and slim because she was not designed to carry the load; her skin is soft and her body is shapely because she was designed to attract a man. Her pelvic is wide and she has a uterus where she carries the man's seed and her offspring can gestate before birth. She was given breast to nurture an infant as she grooms them for life.

This is her God given role, but she is forced to play other rolls so that her children can eat and survive.

She will fight for her children; she will beg for her children; she will serve for her children; she will deny herself and her dignity for her children, and yes, she will even die for her children-some of them die slowly daily, lamenting their children's debacle lives; she dies often of various ailments that often covers a heart that's been broken.

Take a trip into the ghettos of any city, and there you will find homes headed by struggling mamas, hoping and praying that her children make it out.

The black woman's blood covers the black nation from the time they enter the world, and her blood runs richly through our veins.

When we were Negros, we were own by some white man; we were his property; so we were not able to honor our black women like we should. We could not put her in her queenly role and treat her royally with dignity and respect; but, now that we are experiencing a degree of freedom, even in the midst of injustice and prejudice, it is imperative that we recognize and honor our black queens, for they kept us alive and filled with hope when we, as a people, had but died.

The black woman possess the power to lift the black man up to his kingly status; she has the power to empower him to "become" more than he has imagined here-to-fore; she can make him begin to dream again and put dreams in him.

She can make him, once again, lift his head up in pride and dignity and realize that he is somebody. He is a black man out of the belly of a proud people.

The black man, because of his heritage, has endless possibilities buried deep within him; oftentimes buried so deeply that even he doesn't realize his worth.

The black queens words can reestablish him, and build him up once again.

The words that leave the black queen's lips are either pearls or daggers; they can strengthen and they have the power to just as easily kill. She chooses.

She must carefully choose the words that she speaks to her man; taste them before they exit her mouth, for once words are spoken, they can never be withdrawn; and apologies don't remove the damage that has been done.

The black queen must see greatness in him even when he doesn't.

White America has forced the black woman to be by herself, and groomed the black man to shun his responsibilities, and expect menial success or prison.

They put her in the housing projects with other governmental assistance and tell her that she can't have a job or have someone living with her other than her children; and then, they give her a card so that she can take herself and her children to the doctor-physically and psychologically fostering black family without a head-fatherless, husbandless.

Welfare and food stamps hurt the black race more than it helps. It teaches us to depend on somebody else for our wellbeing. The housing projects are designed to keep black people from the American dream-to own their own property.

The system is designed to keep them in the projects. If they get a job and try to help themselves, then their benefits are cut off; so the mentality is that it makes no sense to get a job that won't pay them enough to pay their rent and buy food for their families; not to even mention health care, or day care; so they become stuck in a system that perpetuates itself from one generation to another. Thus, oftentimes, the child develops the mentality of wanting governmental assistance just like mama had.

They are forced to stay in the system, and the system is designed to keep blacks physically and psychologically poor and defeated.

And sadly, as we have stressed, sometimes the achievement hoped for by many of the welfare housing project recipient's children are they hope to be able to get them a governmental housing apartment and a welfare check too; just like their mama while their fathers remain missing in action.

And the ones that want to come out, without proper education, their only option is selling drugs or other illegal activities.

So, the black woman and her children are often caught between a rock and a hard place; they want to do right and get out of the system and become self-sufficient, but the system is designed to keep her and her offspring there-thus limiting what they can do, where they can live, and even how they live.

Thus, they become a product of "heredity plus environment equals behavior". The children that are raised by the system reflect the same.

But, still, I honor and respect the fighting black women, for most of them simply refuse to give up, and fight for their children a better life. They come to understand and teach their children that just because you live in the ghetto, the ghetto doesn't have to live in you. She teaches her children that they have a choice; so even, in substandard housing, and poor living conditions, she teaches her children values, respect, and pride.

The black woman is desperately trying to teach this new generation of young black ladies that are emulating the white women that they don't have to dress half naked to be attractive to a man; that they should leave some parts for their husband's eyes only.

And when you study history, the black woman has always been one of astounding resilience. She is innately moved to protect her children and support her man.

When one observe the black woman around the globe; anywhere that she lives, she is an astoundingly resilient fighter.

In Jamaica, in Haiti, she fights because all comes from that Nubian tribe of blacks out of Egypt in Africa-around the Nile.

When I journeyed to Haiti, I constantly saw the Nubian queens carry big pots of water and other materials balanced atop their heads as they went about their daily business, trying to barter whatever she could to feed her family in one of the poorest nations in the world. She would brave the scorching heat all day trying to sale whatever she could, and then in the evening, comes night fall, she goes home to a make shift hut and cooks for her family the meager means from a hole in the earth.

But, she wouldn't quit; it was in her from her Nubian grandmothers before slavery. I watched many of them sit on a corner in Port A Prince all day with nothing but their hands out, hoping that someone would assist her and her family.

You see, Haiti as well as Jamaica are all descendants of original African slaves. Originally, Haiti was conquered by the French, and Jamaica by the Spanish; but both suffered a slave revolt and were eventually established by the descendants of the slaves-thus, both black countries formed by the descendants of African slaves.

I called them Nubians because all were taken from Africa-all life began in Africa adjacent to Egypt.

It was the Nubian queens that compelled their men to fight and resist, so it is because of her that we have a degree of freedom right now, and if we are to persist, we must entice her to continue to rise up.

Black women birthed the nation, cared for the nation, groomed the nation, and nurtured it-both the blacks and the whites.

During her struggles, as stated previously, she was forced to birth a number of white children too-thus, the people commonly referred to as mulatto. Mr. Charlie's children, but she loved them still, even though her white slave owner had forced his seed deep inside her belly, she still loved them just as much; for she knew that their plight would sometimes be worse than the true blacks for often times they would be disliked by their black relatives because they were too white, and they would be hated by their white relatives because they were too black-thus, their paradox.

She passionately watches the pain in her man's eyes, and feels the struggles he has to deal with day to day with racism and injustice; and with all of her might she pushes him and pushes him until he rises up and grabs hold of his destiny.

Please allow me to pause right here, and say parenthetically that many of our young black women must pull off their pride, and force the black man, that fails to see and fulfill his responsibilities towards his children, to care for his offspring. If he won't volunteer to take care of his children, then, put him in child support. It is a shame that a woman would have to force a man to take care of his own child, but if she has to do that, then she should not hesitate.

The reason why many of our men have settled and ceased to fight is because our Nubian queens have lost their way and their place, and like their European captors, their quest now is dictated by material gain.

She was and always has been truly the force that held us together, for she has always refused to settle, and refused the men in her life to settle. Thus, is the reason why many times she is alone, forced to raise her children by herself because many of the men have settled.

Our black queens, with the tenacity of Rosa Parks that started the civil rights movement when she refused to give up her seat on the city bus to a white man; with the determination of Harriet Tubman that after being freed from slavery, she went back and formed the underground railroad to help free hundreds of other slaves; and with the foresight of Sophia B. Packard that cofounded Spelman college for women; our black mothers refused to quit and sit back and wait until someone else decided to do something for us.

No, she, against all odds, labored forward to save her sons and daughters from hopelessness and a system that unequivocally drowned them in a sea of servitude and injustice from their very birth until they descend the grave.

It is the black woman that has saved the black race from annihilation from without and from within. She saved her people from the white man and from themselves.

She weeps, she prays, she scorns, she fights for her babies, often times alone and many times against the very ones that she conceived from, but still she labors onward, and her only reward is a glimpse of hope and possibilities afforded to her fertile young black beneficiaries.

On the night of 2013, at 10:45, my life forever changed. Mama took her last breath and exited this world forever. Her voice forever silenced. I never really realized how much of a black queen she was until she was gone. My life is forever filled with days that I wish that I could pick up the phone and call for her advice, or just to share with her of my days that is sometimes filled with unrelenting troubles.

And although many times she could do nothing but share bits and pieces of her wisdom, still she soothed me.

Now, there is but silence filled with tears of longing and missing-never really realizing how much she meant to me until she was whiffed away by the angel that shall soon come for us all.

Dr. Akeam Amoniphis Simmons

To all the black queens that sacrificed so much for her babies that just took for granted that she shall always be; the babies that never understood her worth until it was too late, and a gulf was placed between us that neither of us can cross, I salute you and honor you, and ask for your forgiveness for our callous disregard for your true value.

All that we are left with is memories of a black queen that left for too soon!

Sometimes with no lap to rest our head, no soothing voice to ease our pain, and no strong black hands to prop us up, we, as a people, sometimes wonder aimlessly.

Chapter Six

The disappearing black church

The black church, nestled deep inside and into the heart of the black community, through the years, has been a pillar of strength for black people.

The black church was where the black people went to hear from God and receive hope for a better future, and it was often times the meeting place for civil rights activist, and a meeting place to discuss many concerns and ills of the neighborhood.

The black church is where the black man evolved from Negro to "black man"-the black African American that expected the rights and privileges of any American citizen. He wasn't anybody's property to be treated as they wished.

The black church with strong pastors with strong spiritual messages from God taught the black man that he was no longer Negro, America's subservient.

Fiery sermons bellowed from the little, often wooden, pulpit every Sunday morning as streaks of sweat rolled down the pastor's brow and nestled under his chin before he slung it out amidst his jubilantly shouting congregants.

The congregation of fiery black people shed their hurt and tears in worship, if only for a moment, with their God while the rest of their cares waited silently beyond the walls of the church.

They worshipped and praised and brought their heart aches and laid them in the bosom of a loving caring God-Jehovah, who they believed would soon deliver them from their heartless oppressors.

Enthralled in the spirit and deep emotion, they hollered back at the shouting, moaning, hooping, hollering preacher, hoping that God would slay them in the spirit that Sunday morning and give them the strength to endure what they would have to face over and over again the upcoming week-rampant, pervading injustice perpetrated by white America simply because of the color of their skin.

Back then, the pastor didn't always use correct English; his subjects and verbs didn't always agree, and more often than not, he had no seminary training, but he had a heart for God, and a burning passion to spread the delivering truth of God, and to give the people hope of a better day. He warned them of their sins and admonished them to walk in love regardless to how others would treat them.

Many times, the church was a small building that didn't have a bunch of members, and didn't have a lot of money, but their faith in God always rose to the occasion for whatever it was that they were going through.

The pastor's salary was twenty-five to fifty dollars a Sunday-if he got anything at all; that was all that they gave him; no health insurance, no paid vacation, no bonuses, just twenty-five to fifty dollars a Sunday, and sometimes they didn't even raise enough that Sunday to pay the pastor that. But that didn't deter him from returning every Sunday to once again tell them what thus says the Lord.

I look at us now, and I see the traditional black church transforming amidst a torrent of ambiguities of the bible. The black church is disappearing amongst a beguiled thirst and hunger for wealth, only to reappear as this bolshie aristocratic congregation filled with narcissistic bureaucracy that fosters a pervading contagious adamant passion for wealth and prosperity.

They smoothly teach that prosperity is indicative of God's presence and favor. To them, their faith is justified by their state of opulence.

Nestled silently in this new church is the undercurrent of "the Negro" that still wants to be like "Mr. Charlie". He innately thinks that if he can just get God to give him more wealth, stuff, and things, then he would be equal to them; not understanding that white America doesn't care how much money that a black man makes; to them, he's still but a Negro-their former commodity that has lost its value.

But, this new congregation of blacks, refuse to believe or see the truth; so often times they become token members in white congregations, or will watch T.V or social media to absorb that "status"; hoping to become the new aged Negroes; and, they expect their pastors to preach and teach thus so.

When they fail to get this new aged prosperity teaching from the local black pastor, you can hear them saying, "I am not being spiritually fed here" as they exit the building and go join a white congregation, or find a black pastor that will satisfy their craving for the white prosperity doctrine. It's amazing (how can the sheep tell the shepherd what is good food for it or what it wants to eat).

Allow me to pause right here and say that yes, God does bless us, and He is in the blessing business, but He doesn't give wealth without challenge, and often times He brings hope and deliverance through sorrow. You will never truly appreciate the mountain if you haven't yet gone through the valley. Our struggles, our valleys are a very necessary part of our spiritual scope and development. There is little joy without some degree of sorrow.

The Apostle Paul discusses this paradigm principle in the book of 2 Corinthians 11: 23-27. Note what he says:

23. Are they ministers of Christ? (I speak as a fool) I am more; in labors more abundant, in stripes above measure, in prisons more frequent, in deaths oft.

24. Of the Jews five times received I forty stripes save one.

25. Three times was I beaten with rods, once was I stoned, three times I suffered shipwreck, a night and a day I have been in the deep;

26. In journeying often, in perils of water, in perils of robbers, in perils by my own countrymen, in perils by the heathen, in perils in the city, in perils in the wilderness, in perils in the sea, in perils among false brothers.

27. In weariness and painfulness, in watching often, in hunger and thirst, in fasting often, in cold and nakedness.

The Apostle Paul was committed to serving God, and he wrote the preceding passage of the Bible to Illustrate that if you truly serve God, sometimes, often times, you're going to have to go through some things that are not always pleasant. Note, he said that he went hungry sometimes, were beaten sometimes, and put in jail oft-A man of God, hungry-meaning having no food, or not enough food and no money to buy any. But, observe, he glorified God in the end, for he was made perfect through his weakness and what he had to endure.

This is a magnanimous contrast between Paul's church leaders and today's church leaders-the name it and claim it bunch that don't believe that Believers are suppose to have any kind of lack because of their faith.

We must always remember that sometimes God allows troubles to come to help get you out of some troubles that are sometimes unbeknown to you. Lack and need are many times jump start agents in our lives. Like, God sees the cancerous tumor mass in your back, but you feel fine, so He allows some other ailment to come upon you so that you will go to the doctor, and while the doctor is examining one ailment, he finds the cancerous mass in your back just in time before it started to spread.

That is the reason why the Apostle Paul also said that whatever state that he finds himself in, therein he is content.

We must always remember that there is purpose to our pain and sorrow, but Jehovah is always working it out. He does what is best for us.

One of the problems with today's black church is perpetuating a false sense of security through "having more". Its members have developed an acute barrage of solipsism where their main focus is on themselves.

I hear their preachers, prophets, preaching to them that they are going to acquire more, be more, and get rich so to prove to the world that they are the blessed of the Lord.

Very rarely do you hear their preacher telling them of their sins, and the cost of sins, or how to be victorious even while in despair; no they tell them what they shall have (what they want to hear-inching ears). Malcolm X called it being "hood winked".

The black today's church is desperately trying to emulate the white congregation with their partisan multipurpose endeavors that is geared mainly towards prosperity, and while prosperity is good, it cannot stand by itself; else one will have wealth but no heart; substance with no compassion or empathy-empty religion.

The black church must return to its significance, a dual purpose of getting the people ready to stand before God, and helping the community rise out of despair. The neighborhood is supposed to benefit from the presence of the church being amongst them; one of the churches purpose is to elevate the community and make it better.

Our fight, our struggles, and our pains, are supposed to be addressed from our pulpits; for our pews are filled with pain and wounded parishioners that's silently screaming and crying for help.

We need to know how to live holy and whole, and how to come together as a community and help one another. Every other race of people that comes to the United States does it-the Chinese come together; the Italians come together; the Indians come together, the Koreans come together; it is far past time that the black people begin coming together, and the black community church can greatly help this effort.

Yes, we must supersede those sound good sermons that are filled with sound good hooping and hollering that leave us feeling good but empty-the services that makes us leave the same way that we came-defeated.

Our problem today in the black church is that the pastors, particularly this present and younger generation, has reverted back and grabbed hold of the Negro mentality to whereby he wants to be just like Mr. Charlie, the white pastor. His drive is to acquire a larger congregation-several congregation.

The all pervading substance in his sermons is prosperity and God's material blessings, so sub sequentially, many of his parishioners, to prove that God is blessing them, will go out and buy stuff that they cannot afford-to give a visage of prosperity. Thus, they go out and buy a Cadillac only to have to park it in a space in the government projects.

This pastor, with the Negro mentality, congregants learn all too soon that prosperity by itself will not deliver the black race from injustice.

We must also be taught the value of social strength, and political strength. Our pastor cannot afford the Negro state of mind-to be just like Mr. Charlie-the white man; for it is detriment to our survival.

The slave Negro mentality is not gotten rid of overnight, or in a few years. Even though all of the blacks today, were never slaves, nor were their grandfathers, or their great grandfathers, still we suffer from the ailments passed down through many generations from our long ago forefathers that were slaves for over two hundred years.

It just seems logical and stands to reason that if a race of people were in slavery for over two hundred years, then, it would appear that they would need nearly as much time to adjust and adapt to their new found freedom. Many were born into slavery; that was all that they knew.

You see, therein lies the problem that I have with some of the statements made by those black people that disagree with President Trumps immigration policies, where he wants to deport all "illegal immigrants." I stress illegal. For, as I have fore stated, some blacks readily state that we black folks use to be illegal immigrants too, but I beg to differ. Blacks were never illegal immigrants. They never came here illegally be themselves; they didn't sneak across the border to get into the United States. No, black people were a commodity brought back as a piece of property, like any other piece of property that the white man had ordered from overseas.

The black church has an awesome responsibly; while it is a place of worship and exaltation to our God, and a place to hear from the Lord, its mission is still to keep the black congregants focused, and on track. The pastors must train his parishioners of acquiring **economical strength**, **political strength**, and **social strength**. We cannot allow ourselves to be so heavenly focused until we become no earthly good. We ought to have some heaven while living on earth.

Economical strength:

The white society only respects money and power-power in those three areas. If black people have economical strength, then they will have learned how to pool the billions of dollars that they collectively make each year. They will build their own banks, their own supermarkets, their own car dealerships, their own restaurants, and shopping plazas and shopping malls. Black enterprise would thrive.

To acquire **economical strength**, blacks must patronize black businesses. Yes, you might can get a cheaper price at the bigger white merchant down the street because he can offer you a cheaper price because he buy in bulk, and because he is bigger, his selection is larger.

We must resist being lured off to other store at given times. They always ascribe a reason why the black man should bring his money to them. They will have a white sale; a black sale; the black Friday sale; a Christmas sale, and the day after Christmas sale. Then, there is the Easter sale, and Halloween ....etc..... etc......etc......etc..... Every holiday that you can think of has a sale-which is really not a sale at all.

They trick the consumers; which is the reason why their sales pitch has changed over time. Now, they no longer emphasizes how much an item costs-house, automobile, furniture, appliances, jewelry- they avoid the total cost and have you only focus on the **monthly payment.** 600.00 a month sounds a whole lot better than, "The price of the car is 40.000." Or, like if you buy a 200.000.00 house, and you are excited because you are financing it at 3%, but what most don't realize is that they are really paying more than 3% interest. It is only 3% if you pay it off in one year, which would have you paying a little over 207,000.00 for your house, but in reality, after thirty years, you will have paid over 333,000.00 for your

200.00.00 house. You will have paid over a 133.000.00 in interest alone, and the price escalates when the interest is higher.

They give you one sale after another to lure you in to spend your hard earned money often times on somethings that you don't even need.

Many times, the sales are not really sales at all, but prices that they have lowered only after having jacked them up.

White America acquire and maintain economical power because they always find a way to get our money, and if they have it, then there is none or very little for our own communities. They get you to believe that you've got to have the latest Mercedes Benz, the latest Cadillac, the latest BMW, or whatever high end car that suits your taste.

White America convinces black people, through advertisement, that they have got to wear a certain kind of shoes, or dress, or hat; and they convince black women that they have got to carry a certain kind of purse that cost several hundred dollars- only to have no money in the purse.

All of this is done by us to make us look like the white folks; which, in turns, generates more wealth for them and keeps black America poverty stricken; thus, living in substandard housing, but driving an expensive car and dressed in expensive clothes and shoes.

STOP AND TURN AROUND!!!!! WE MUST DEVELOP GENERATIONAL WEALTH SO THAT WE CAN GIVE OUR CHILDREN A JUMP START!!!!!!!

For our merchandise needs, we must support black businesses that are oftentimes struggling to make it because we refuse to patronize them; instead, we take our business to those that will not sow back into our neighborhoods.

The small black business cannot compete with them because most of our people have not been taught the bigger picture.-black enterprise saves and exalt black people. To lift ourselves up economically, we cannot afford to wait for somebody else to do it. It is incumbent upon us to save us.

Instead of always going to those high end, upscale restaurants, or your regular general restaurants, go over to mom and pop's small restaurant to support them.

Yes, I practice this; I go across town to a small mama's restaurant; it is a whole in the wall place, but it is clean and the food is good, and I know that she appreciates my business, and that she is trying to come up out of the norm of working for somebody else to little end. Instead of going to the mega book stores, go support the little black owned book store uptown or down town. Go out of your way to sow into your own garden; if they don't have what you are looking for, they can order it just like the larger book stores.

Patronize our clothing stores, for they specialize in what we like; sometimes, you might have to go out of your way, but it is worth helping our people come up. We must support our own businesses and enterprises if we are to acquire much needed economical strength.

No one respects you very much if you are broke-it is the American way, which is the reason why they implemented the Credit Scoring system to realize quickly what's your worth to them.

Political Strength

we must build ourselves **political strength**-a basis to give us political power. Though our political system has much to be desired, still, we have no clout without a political voice. It has been proven time and time again that the black vote matters, that the ballot can make a difference.

They recognize you when they need your vote; they will invite you to the table of change when they need your vote, and what you say matters to them when you have a vote for which they need.

We must become a political machine that they must recon with. We must choose the candidates that serve our best interest; and those that are in office, we must not forget, during voting time, which politician helped us most, and the ones that didn't serve us at all. We make the difference for ourselves and our children. Politicians only concern is votes, particularly when reelection is imminent.

We must remain vigilant and adamant to our cause, and must not allow ourselves to become relaxed and comfortable with what we have achieved thus far-the greatest is yet to come.

Yes, our country has passed laws, but many times fail to keep them. In 1865, the United States passed the law to free all slaves and made slavery illegal. In 1866, a bill was passed, in spite of the president's veto-president Andrew Jackson, stating that all people born in the United States are citizens-which made the slaves that were born in the United States, American citizens, and on February third in 1869, the United States passed a bill that gave all black men the right to vote.

So there, the black man-ex-slave was freed, made a citizen, and given the right to vote-in the 1800s; but almost one hundred years later, the black man was still struggling for his freedom, citizenship, and right to vote. It was virtually hypocrisy in our nation, for they made laws on paper but didn't enforce them in real life from state to state.

One hundred years later, in September 9, 1957, the United States enacted the voting rights bill which was the first Federal Civil Rights legislation passed by the nation's congress since the Civil Rights act of 1875. This law was designed to give the justice department, federal prosecutors, court injunctions against interference with the right to vote.

One hundred years later, the Civil Rights act of 1964 was passed by congress, which ended segregation in public places, and banned employment discrimination on the basis of race, creed, color, sex, religion, or national origin.

One hundred years later, the Civil Rights act of 1968 was passed; it was the fair housing act. It provided for equal housing opportunities regardless of race, sex, religion, or national origin.

So, why would all of these bills have to be passed one hundred years later after the United States government had already freed the black man, made him a citizen, and gave him the right to vote-all in the 1800s.

They didn't inforce their laws; they decided to enforce them one hundred years later, but still, the masses of white America did not want this freedom and equal rights privileges for the black people; which is why Medgar Evens was killed in 1963, shot in his front yard after arriving home from a NAACP meeting. He fought and lost his life trying force white America to adhere to their laws.

On February 21, 1965, Malcolm X was killed in New York while he gave a speech; he fought for the pursuit of equal rights for black people.

And, on April 4, 1968, Martin Luther King was killed in Memphis Tennessee because he too fought for America to keep the laws of civil rights for all of its people.

All of them rallied and shed their blood while giving their life for the black man to have rights through the political scene, which would bring him equal rights in all areas.

Medgar evens stated emphatically that the black people's only hope is the control the vote.

Often times, the only time that the black man is counted and listened to is during voting time. Considering these changing times, it is imperative that we possess political worth. We must barter with the ones that is seeking office for what is best for us and our interest.

The black race must not allow the white special interest groups and politicians to choose for us; no, we must do our homework and pay attention to the candidates and know what is at stake, for therein lies the truth sometimes tucked away and hidden amongst all of the tinsel of candidacy where truth is often filtered and shaped by a party.

Our political strength must become pooled and collective as one unit to uplift our candidate. It is how we put Barrack Obama in office. We came out as one unit to make history by helping to put the first black president of the United States of America in office. We, as a black people couldn't even imagine such a thing twenty years ago, or even ten years ago, but black people came together and fought their cause.

After the election of Barrack Obama, black folks, once again slipped back into lackadaisicalness, and wait for the white man to give us who he see fit for us, but it's not really for us, but for his own self-motivated purposes.

Social Strength

Lastly, and perhaps, most importantly, black people must have **social strength**, for without social strength, you can never fully acquire economical and political strength. Social strength is relating to each other, caring about it other. It is helping each other rise to the occasion and make a better world for each other. We must transcend that idiosyncratic way that is built upon solipsism and narcissism, and be concern about our fellow man, whether he is next door to us, or across town. We all share a common bond. We will all rise up together, or we shall all perish together. Those shipmen that are in the bow of the ship cannot afford to not be concern about those sailors in the stern of the ship if the ship is burning and sinking, for in saving them, we save ourselves.

Black people cannot afford to wait on congress to stop the drive by shootings, violence, and drug dealing in our neighborhoods; we must do that for ourselves. The White House is bombarded with its own problems.

As it has been said on numerous occasions before, congress can pass laws, but they cannot legislate love. We don't have the luxury to sit back and hope and wait for someone to love us enough to treat us right and give us justice and equality.

Booker T. Washington knew that when he said that blacks and whites, in America can operate together and separately; he said that we can be as together as the hand, but as divided as the fingers-socially take care of ourselves. He was stressing that we had allowed ourselves to become too dependent upon our former captors-to work things out for us and provide for us. We need not a hand out, but a hand up, then, we'll reach back and give another brother a hand up until all of us are up and out.

Marcus Garvey stress that we as black people should go back to Africa because he thought that the black man could not truly ascertain justice and equality in America. He thought that white America would never see black people as true citizens of the United State. The United States were willing and ready to get rid of the Negro, for the Negro reminded them of their own inhumane behavior; so they bought land in West Africa and called it Liberia-a place in Africa where ex-slaves could go "back home".

But, the problem was, now the ex-slave's descendants are no longer ex-slaves; America was all that they knew, so there was no "going back"; they were home right here in the United States-born and raised.

The same is true with Malcolm X. Most think that Malcolm X was assassinated by the Nation of Islam, and while members of the Nation of Islam might have pulled the trigger; it was ordered and coerce by the hidden powers that be. Malcolm X assassination was a political one. He was killed because he wanted to make the black people's plight one of "human rights" rather than "civil rights". You see, Malcom X knew that as long as we were labored as civil rights, then our fight remain a home fight within our own nation, and only expected to be dealt with by our nation. Malcolm X, rightly so, argued that it was a denial of our human rights, and if it left being civil rights, and went to being a cause of human rights, then Malcolm X could take the black American injustice before other nations of the world, and get assistance globally from other nations around the world-the hidden powers could not let that happen!

No one is going to do for us if we fail to attempt to do for ourselves. We know who the shooters are in our community. It is time for us to speak up and put those that rob and kill in the neighborhoods in jail. You don't have to go and chase anyone down; just if **you see something** criminal, **say something**, and report it. Our babies are being gunned down in the streets while walking to school, and some are even shot by a stray bullet while sleeping at home in their own beds. **It has to stop!!**

If we don't care, they won't care. No one is going to do for you that for which you can do for yourself.

We don't want to say it or admit it, but our children are out of control, which they acquired from the privileged white kids. They are like that partly because we are scared to discipline them because white America wants our children to be just as disrespectful as theirs; they make laws saying that you can't spank your child because it is child abuse, so we, as parents no longer spank our children, therefore, little Johnny becomes uncontrollable.

Because he is not controlled at home, he cannot be controlled at school- in the class room, they make a special class just for him; they call it Special Education, or special Ed, which labels the child for the rest of his academic life. Mine you, special Ed is just a holding cell until he becomes of age where they can put him in a jail cell most of his adult life.

It all stems from a lack of home discipline. You cannot expect the teachers to raise your child; you must do that at home. And, "time out" (where you tell the child to stand in a corner with his face against the wall for a few minutes) doesn't work-sometimes he needs a whipping.

The bible further discusses it, note: Proverbs 23: 13-14:

13. Withhold not correction from the child: for if you beat him with the rod, he shall not die.

14. You shall beat him with the rod, and shall deliver his soul from hell.

Note again what the bible says of whipping your child: Proverbs 13: 24

24. He that spares his rod hates his son: but he that loves him chastens him all the time.

In other words, as the old cliché goes, stare the rod, spoil the child.

We cannot rightly be angry at the school system because they refuse to allow our children to pray at school-though I wish that they would, when we don't even show them how to or make them pray at home.

Our children build our communities; they are our present and our future.

We must take pride in our communities, and be connected to each other; stop letting our house fall apart, and letting dilapidated houses and businesses rest amongst us like eye sores and become lounging places for dope.

Our lack of keeping our neighborhoods clean and refurbished, perhaps goes back to the Negro slavery days when he lived in an old shack while Mr. Charlie lived in the nice big white house on the hill. The Negro, ex-slave, lived as he was supposed to. But, that mentality must change amongst our people, in our communities. Remove those cars that sitting in the front yard jacked up on bricks, and remove the other old cars or trucks that is not running and just sitting around your house. Paint your house, and keep your front yard neat, clean, and cut; for this will only maintain and increase your property value.

Most cities that you visit, you can tell when you enter its black communities because of the lack of care. You often see junk cars-several of them sitting in and around the yard. Everywhere you turn, you will see many houses that are unkempt and badly in need of care.

Sometimes I think that black communities that are in disrepair have more often been orchestrated by the white establishment because if you will notice, most cities, particularly large cities, improve, rebuild and update their towns, but the black neighborhoods, sitting right adjacent to their new developments, are passed over and ignored; so, in essence, what they have is a thriving city with a decrepit black community nestled not far from it-hidden just a few blocks over nestled upon the old adage that says out sight, out of mind.

In Birmingham Alabama, they have a black mayor, a black police chief, a black superintendent, and a mostly black city council; the inner city, down town is thriving, but yet the black communities are ravaged by high crime-murder, drugs, and the sort. Note, many of the murders go unsolved. It's as though they push the black communities under the rug and never to be remembered until election time, then, they are bombarded by gross promises that they already know that they don't intend to fulfill unless, of course, the problem spills over into the white communities.

But, when the problems spill over into the white communities, it is treated differently.

For instance, as long as crack and heroin, and opioids were in the black neighborhood, White America's solution for it was make stricter laws, build bigger prisons, and put them in jail; when the drug epidemic spilled over into the white folks neighborhood, they started referring to the drug usage as a sickness that needed to be treated. They assert that the users don't need prison time, but therapy and counseling-not more and bigger prisons, but understanding judges and police officers.

It's called white privilege!

This would not be tolerated in the white communities-not for a moment.

It happens over and over again, from Detroit to Florida, white America will often go in and buy up the town, and buy out the blacks, then build new Condos, stores, businesses. Then, later, if the black man wanted to move back to the area where he grew up, he can't because he can't afford it. Yes, the law says that you can live where ever you want to, but they price you out.

We must come together and unite as one. As the old African proverbs say, "It takes a whole village to raise one child." In other words, the black people must become one. All of us must become concern about all of us.

The black church must return to being a hub in the community, and our pastors must be deeper than whether his socks match his tie, or what kind of suit he has on, or what kind of car that he drives.

It is incumbent upon our churches to remain a place for the weary, the mistreated, the hurting, the wounded, the disenchanted, and the ones who have just come to believe that they don't matter; all amidst their heavy burden of lost and a piercing feeling of the agony of defeat.

The church must lead us back to connecting with one another, and trying to help meet our needs, both spiritually and physically as the church did in the 1940s.

In the 1940s, when the black soldiers came back home from the war, white banks refused to give them a loan to buy a house for their families; even though they had risked life, health, and death to save this country and keep it free from communist or any other foreign enemy, when they came back home to the United States, they were judged by the color of their skin rather than the content of their character. The banks refused to give them a loan to buy a house.

But, the church stepped in and started a credit union and allowed the black veterans to buy themselves a home for their families. The churches opened up a credit union that allowed the soldiers to borrow up to five times what they had deposited.

Yes, the church must come alive again in the black community and reach out a hand to its neighbors to guide them back to a conscious of holiness, clean living, and pride.

The black church has to be more than just a place of worship, of coming to sing and dance and shout unto the Lord; it has to become and remain a catalyst for change, and a refuge for the hurting, both spiritually and physically.

Jesus defined the scope of the church in Luke 4: 18; note:

The Spirit of the Lord is upon me, because he has anointed me to preach the gospel to the poor; he has sent me to heal the broken hearted, to preach deliverance to the captives, and recovering of sight to the blind, to set at liberty them that are bruised.

The church is supposed to bring hope to the masses, and help them that are psychologically blind, to see. It is to instruct them in the Good News of change, so that their hearts, that life has broken, can be healed............ That's the church!

We must rid ourselves of those pulpit pimps that are feeding our flesh with empty dreams and fantasies of a life without struggle.

When we receive that teaching that tells us that an indication of our blessed state is the material things that we have, to prove this, we often go out and purchase things that we cannot afford.

Chapter Seven

Changing the way we think

Whether Black, White, Asian, Hispanic, or any other nationality or ethnic group, we are all the end result of what we constantly think of ourselves and the world around us; this process is called Our Level of Consciousness.

The bible says that as a man thinks, then so is he. Jesus reiterated this point when He said that out of a man's hearth, flows the issues of life. If we want to change our surroundings, our city, our nation, and even our world, we must first change our level of thinking, thereby, changing our perception of things.

We can even change bad events to good ones when we changed the way we perceive them to be. An example of this is the piercing of a man's ears. While we look at it as something glamorous today, its original conception was to announce a man's voluntary enslavement forever. It was to show everybody that saw him that he was somebody else's slave forever. Note Exodus 21: 5-6:

5. And if the servant shall plainly say, I love my master, my wife, and my children; I will not go out free:

6. Then his master shall bring him unto the judges; he shall also bring him to the door, or unto the door post; and his master shall bore his ear through with an awl; and he shall serve him forever.

Observe what it says of a man's ear piercing in Deuteronomy 15: 13-17:

13. And when you send him out free from you, you shall not let him go away empty:

14. You shall furnish him liberally out of your flock, and out of your floor, and out of your winepress: of that wherewith the Lord your God has blessed you you shall give unto him.

15. And you shall remember that you was a bondman in the land of Egypt, and the Lord your God redeemed you: therefore I command you this thing today.

16. And it shall be, if he says unto you, I will not go away from you; because he loves you and your house, because he is well with you;

17. Then you shall take an awl, and thrust it through his ear unto the door, and he shall be your servant forever. And also unto your maidservant you shall do likewise.

So, you see now, that for a man to have an earpiece in his ears, signifies that he is somebody else's slave; he belongs to someone else for as long as he lives-and it means that he willingly chose to be an eternal slave!

But, over the years, we changed our perception of pierced ears, and made it seem good, and something to be acceptable, but truth is, it signifies that you are somebody's slave forever.

They put diamonds in the ear's hole; gold in the ear's hole, and all kinds of other things to dress up the hole in the ear, but it still doesn't change what it means-the bearer is somebody else's property, somebody else's slave forever.

The end result is still the same; we just changed the way that we see things. We changed our way of thinking of the matter.

We can never change our environment without first changing our thought process-our level of consciousness-how we receive it and how re react and relate to it.

You can free the slave, but if his mind is still the save, he is yet a slave bound to be servant to someone else.

Like the preachers that visited the White House, in August of 2018, and sat down to collectively talk to President Trump; they sat there with their slave mentality. They were so glad to be in the presence of Mr. Charlie, and under the lime light until they failed to represent the people or present the troubles that are plaguing the black community.

One of them said to President Trump that He was so thankful to the president for having a heart for black people; another of them said to President Trump that he was glad to be there because President Trump was the most pro-black president that we have ever had; on and on those preacher went on sucking up and kissing up, I am thinking to myself, "Huh! What!".

During the back lash for their actions, they tried to justify their lack of representation by stating that other men of God went and sat down with the various kings in the bible, and I wanted to say to them, yes they did, but they didn't go kissing up; they went to help the people.

Can you hear Moses telling Pharaoh, "We're so thankful that you have a heart for the people-making them strong by working the hell out of them."

That was a shameful day for the black church when a few opportunistic preachers decided to go and attempt to gain prestige at the cost of the black community.

I am not altogether berating them, for I suspect that all of us can be overwhelmed by the lime light, and become star struck. It is just human nature.

We all will put our foot in our mouths from time to time, and say something so utterly crazy until when we reflect back upon our conversations, we are flabbergasted and bewildered at how and why we made such statements.

If we expect relevant change in our communities, those that go to the White House must honestly attempt to lay our cause out to the President-the injustice, the police brutality, the discrimination, the disparity amongst the black citizen of the United States....ect....ect.....ect.

Our mindset has to change even in the pulpit, for often times the pulpit feeds the people.

If you see yourself as nothing, then you become nothing. It is oftentimes taught that opposites attract, but I beg to differ. You will always attract what you are, or what you "believe" yourself to be. The universe demands that we attract that which is most like ourselves. It is in our DNA-we are attracted to those that are most like us.

In the twelfth chapter of Genesis, Jehovah told Abram to get out from amongst his kindred. He wasn't referring just to his relatives, although they are not entirely excluded; no, He was talking about those folks, their bad habits and way of thinking that he has constantly been around.

God was giving Abram a new level of consciousness that he would not fully receive if he remained around his present constituents. Those that you surround yourself with will have the most influence on you.

I think I am royal, therefore, royalty comes to me.

If you want to be debt free someday, it is paramount that you leave those folks with the mindset that believes that it is natural for you to owe someone all of your life.

Most cities that you visit, you can tell when you enter into the Hood. The houses are usually dilapidated, with broken down cars that are sometime resting on bricks with unkempt yards and trash along the streets. Substandard supermarkets and convenient stores usually ran by foreigners. Yes, it is the Hood. Of course, there are a few exceptions to the rule, but the level of consciousness is "just let it go", and the vendors seem to think to give them substandard products because they won't care.

You see, when you start thinking better and differently, your entire world changes. It evolves to accommodate the way that you think and the way that you see yourself.

It does not matter how many opportunities that you have if you fail to see them as opportunities. It's only an opportunity if you siege the moment.

One of the most powerful gifts that the black man has is his ability to adjust, accept, adopt, and rationalize his present state of being. Therefore, he can become satisfied with most given circumstances—no matter how depraved and unjust they are. We can become comfortable even with the least of things, and will become angry and up-set with anyone that will attempt to change where we are.

Some people can become so comfortable on the bottom until they get angry at anyone that attempts to change their way of life.

This is the premise that our government fails to understand. Yes, you can give them food stamps, and housing projects, but if you fail to enhance their level of thinking about themselves, then you only deepen their problem-even sometimes to several generations.

I have seen to whereby the government goes in to the housing projects and paint the building a pretty color, plant flowers in the yards, and put security at the front entrance, but fail to invest in their level of thinking and how they think about themselves.

So, in just a short while, they will rewrite graffiti all over the buildings, pluck up the flowers, sell their food stamps, and breach the front entrance security.

If inside, one sees themselves as substandard or nothing, then one will make their surroundings a self fulfilling prophecy of themselves-one is a reflection of the other.

The black man's biggest problem is not the white man or any other race of people; his problem lies in how he thinks of himself. The white slave owner knew this, that's why the first things that he did to the newly acquired slave is change his name and culture so the slave forgot who he was, and if you fail to know who you are, then you will readily accept who someone says you are.

Like the hole in the eternal slave's ear, our reality becomes then, what we perceive it to be. Thus, is the reason why black folks chemically fry their hair, color their eyes, and bleach their skin; because subconsciously they have been taught that Caucasian features are beautiful, they do all they can to become as white as they can. And, the white world constantly sends us subliminal messages of the "rightness" of white.

If I am to change the world, I must first change how I see the world. Most are waiting for a change, but you must become aggressive and make the change. It starts with each individual.

We must grasp for a new level of consciousness; a consciousness that reaches higher and further outside of our on box of life.

We must become uncomfortable with where we are, and seek to change and achieve better for ourselves and our children. We must invest in posterity.

If we, as a people, don't change our thought process, our children have little chance of continued and elevated success.

Thinking is what separates man from beast.

I think, therefore, I am. I am the end result of all that I think. The things that I think of are attracted to me, and become my reality.

My language is intimately connected to my thinking. I think it; I speak it, and I act and react according to my thought process.

Our thinking process is the reason why one man will fight, and another man will flee, and yet even another man will yield and quickly surrender and obey.

We must abate that Negro thinking mentality. The Negro thinks of himself as less, therefore, he is subservient to all and belligerent to all that looks like him, because, deep down in his subconscious mind, he really doesn't like being a Negro-somebody's property; and, the white world never ever seize to remind him that he was once their commodity, therefore, they feel that the black man is overtly less than them.

It does not matter how educated he is or what his job status is, or even if he has a six figure income, the white establishment still sees the black man as less.

It is just the opposite with white folk; it matters not of how little education they have, or having a menial job, or unemployed, and they could live in a shack in the woods, but they will still feel that they are better than the black man because he is a negro which psychologically resonates to them that he is less; even though the black man is more educated, has a better job, lives in a better neighborhood, he is still less to them.

This superiority complex personality was taught to them from their very beginning, and is constantly subliminally taught to them every day as they mature-society indoctrinates them to believe that they are better.

So, the only one that can change the black man's plight in society is the black man, and the very first thing that he must do is pull off his negro labelling, for it is his greatest liability, but it is not so easily done; for it is not just a labelling; it is a way of thinking and of living.

In order for the black man to change his thinking process, he must have or adamantly acquire and maintain at least four levels of sight; they are:

1. **PRESENT SIGHT**
2. **HINDSIGHT**
3. **FORESIGHT**
4. **INSIGHT**

Let's take a closer look at these four levels of sight that is pertinent to the black man's continued growth and escape from white mental slavery:

1. **Present sight:** is the ability to see things as they truly are.

   The black man must have vision and the ability to envision. If one fails to see things as they are, one can never change their environment. Denying where you are will not change where you are. You only lie to yourself.

We are discriminated against; we reap seeds of injustice that we didn't sow, and this has been permitted to persist for so long until it has change our present sight-the way that we see things in our personal lives; in our day to day environment.

Because our present sight is saturated with an onslaught of callous sentiments of "who" we are, we attack each other just as quickly as the racist do.

The Negro is often blinded by where he is. He thinks that he is alright and everything is good because he can wear the expensive shoes, suits, and accessories that the white man made for him. It is like the share cropper used to be. He thought that he owned part of the land, so he worked the land throughout the year thinking that he would be rewarded at the end; only to find out when pay day came, he got nothing, or very little because he owed Mr. Charlie for goods that he had purchased on credit throughout the year; even oftentimes owing Mr. Charlie. It happened so long until it became accepted.

You see, if your present sight becomes doctored, then you will not see the present and what position you are in. You will only see what has been presented to you-You are doing alright because you wear expensive sneakers, suits, drive an expensive car, and live in a house that you usually can't afford; that becomes your present sight which is an illusion.

It is the magic syndrome. We all know that there is no such thing as magic, and that the magician is merely a clever trickster, but still, we are fascinated by being tricked, even though we know that it is not real-he is tricking us.

Over the years, the Negro has been duped and tricked to believe that things are good where he is, and that he should be satisfied and be happy with things the way that they are, for after all, it is not as bad as it used to be.

It is imperative that I see where I am, thus I can adjust and shift myself to make provisions for where I need to be.

I can never move higher unless I see my present situation in real time; see it for what it is, and not what the political magician told me it is.

The Negro present sight is severely altered, or how else could you explain them wearing a sign that says "black lives matter" when, in essence, we are filling the funeral home with black bodies; so then, the question becomes, "does black lives matter to black people.

Change always starts with the individual, and then spreads abroad. The masses will never change unless the individual changes first, and the individual will not change unless he first realize the true state of his present condition or situation.

Our present sight must be real. We must take off the blinders that the establishment has placed upon us, and see where we are, then, and only then, will we be able to see something else.

That is what separates black people now from our forefathers; they never lost sight of where they were, and the conditions that they were in. Yes, they were Negroes, but they always desired a change because they didn't like what they presently saw.

Note, where you are, then you can see clearly to determine where you destine to be.

HINDSIGHT: The ability to look back, and see where we came from; what we have gone through, and where we have been.

If you don't know where you came from, then, you cannot appreciate where you are, and lose sight of where you should be, or want to be.

One of the greatest problem with this present generation is that they have forgotten where they came from, and the elders are desperately trying also to forget. We have ceased to teach our children their heritage; thus, they fail to understand the struggles that afforded us this degree of prosperity and freedom that we presently have-no matter how marginal it may appear to be.

A lot of blood was shed; a lot of lives were lost to propel the black race out of the Negro status, but the masses forgot, or never knew it because this generation is disillusioned by material gain; thus, their heritage is ingrained into someone else's heritage while they deny their own.

It equates to someone else looking through your rear view mirror and telling you what you should see. This is the reason why many Negroes celebrate Emancipation Proclamation, not really understanding that it was a strategy of war rather than merely an act to free the slaves.

Because they have little hindsight is the reason why Negroes celebrate the fourth of July-America's celebrating freedom from Britain. Why should black folk celebrate? We were still slaves then. America gained its freedom in 1776; the slaves were freed in 1865.

Negroes live but mediocre and unfulfilled destinies without proper hindsight-the ability to understand and know from whence one came.

Our past is rich and saturated with African culture, heritage, and pride-some even filled with royalty.

If we forget our past, then we become but Negroes whose been defined by the white man who was often our oppressor, and the oppressor never has the best interest of the oppressed at the forefront of his mind.

We must look back and see the power of our strong black women and determined black men who would sometimes have their feet cut off because they continued to try to escape-refused to accept continuing to be somebody's property.

Hindsight makes black people understand that we didn't get the degree of freedom that we have by our own work, but rather, we are where we are because we stand proudly, and sometimes ignorantly upon the shoulders of a proud relentless people-Black grandmothers and granddaddies, mamas and daddies that struggled and endured much suffering to afford their children a better world; even though many of them never tasted the sweet nectar of equality and civil rights themselves.

We owe it to our ancestors to be a proud God fearing people that appreciates the bloodshed and struggles that our forefathers went through because they thought more of us than of themselves.

They didn't just have sympathy for their future offspring, but they had much empathy-not wanting their future babies to be enslaved, lynched, and discriminated against with no justice or civil rights. No, they fought and died to give their future generations a better life.

I think that this generation of blacks have little hindsight and little appreciation for their ancestral past is partly, but not completely, due to the fact that more of our babies are having babies; therefore, grandparents are younger-there is a distinct difference between a grandmother that is in her thirties, and a grandmother that is in her sixties.

The grandmother doesn't want to be old; so she acts young and has a young person's disposition. Some things are essential that we acquire from those that went before us.

We must never forget the struggles that was encountered and endured before us.

We must acquire the resilience, the determination, and pride of our forefathers, and have hindsight enough to remember the fight.

FORESIGHT: The ability to predict or the action of predicting what will happen or be needed in the future-the act or power of foreseeing.

If the black man allows himself to remain a Negro, then he is ultimately destined to regress back to the old American slave that is simply some white man's property.

We must have foresight enough to chart our own course, and do the things that are needed to produce the changes that we desire.

The black man will not just accidently wonder into a better life, or wonder into justice, equality, and civil rights. No, he must predict what will happen, and produce the actions needed to materialize his desired results.

He does not have the luxury to sit back and enjoy the little comforts of "right now" which was afforded him by his forefathers.

The black man must chart his own path down roads of prosperity for himself and his offspring.

Prosperity has little worth without being enveloped and saturated with the thoughts of posterity.

Every generation stands upon the shoulders of its predecessors.

We are the end result of the mind-set of our fathers before us; which is the reason I am severely concerned about the generations succeeding the millennial's.

If we are superficial and only care about material things and stuff, then we only leave our children to inherit shallow benefits.

That is the essential thing that differed the Negro from his owner; he has little foresight. He sees and accepts what white society tells him of himself.

White folks always endeavor to leave their children something to help propel them forth when their demise has come and they have to cross over into that land called death.

It's called generational wealth-old money.

We curse our succeeding generation when we fail to have the foresight enough to help them try and go further than we ourselves have gone.

Lack of foresight is the reason why some Negroes will live their entire lives in a governmental housing project-never even thinking of some day owning their own house. Some will live in an apartment, and always be satisfied with what they believe is a "nice" apartment.

There is an old lady, in the town where I grew up, that lives in a very small compact duplex apartment. It has a very small living room; a very little bed room, and a closet of a kitchen. She has rented that little place every since I can remember from a little boy. Thus, she has rented that little duplex for over sixty years.

Renters love people like her who has no foresight to imagine someday owning her own house. Sixty years of renting the same house! Over the years, she has paid for the entire duplex several times over, and yet remain satisfied paying rent. She has no foresight.

Foresight is simply peering off into your future and imagining the end result; and although it is tomorrow, in the future, you endeavor to influence it today. Do, right now, those things needed to give your future the outcome you desire.

Dr. Akeam Amoniphis Simmons

Do now what you have to do until later when you can do what you want to do.

Influence tomorrow's dreams today, and one can only achieve this by foresight.

INSIGHT: The ability to gain an accurate and deep understanding of a person or thing. It is to understand what has happened to us; how we got where we are, and what is happening to the black man right now.

Insight amongst us is understanding why it is imperative that we seize and desist being Negroes and truly and rightly embrace who we are and where we came from so that we can embrace our destiny.

We are black Americans whose veins are rich with African blood.

Insight is understanding why the white supremest, the KKK, the fascist, and even the liberals determine themselves to be inherently better than the black man, and why they endeavor to keep him a subservient Negro.

And, mind you, all white folks that don't like black folks are not all inherently evil racist.

No one likes anything that reminds them of their shortcomings, ugly ways, or past evil deeds. They cannot portray themselves as good and righteous as long as they are face to face with someone that they have wronged.

The black face reminds him of his evil ways, and the ungodly things that he has done to a people simply to fulfill his own thirst for gain.

Insight Is knowing the full story, and responding accordingly.

If the black man fails to have present sight, hindsight, foresight, and insight, then, he will fail to have the right vision; and without the right vision, he will never envision what is best for himself, thereby, remaining simply a Negro that waits for white America to come to his aid with a handout; not realizing that the handouts are designed to keep him where he is.

Note, the governmental housing projects are designed to keep their tenants in the projects and on welfare. Observe, one cannot live there unless they make substandard wages, and one is not permitted to earn more while living there or else they are evicted. So thus, they force to recline to stay where they are-being cared for by the white establishment-still a Negro that Mr. Charley is taking care of.

It is too expensive to remain a Negro; it cost our children too much; but, we cannot do way with our Negro status unless we change our thinking process.

Whatever I think that I am, I become. I think it, therefore I am it.

Chapter Eight

The quest for inclusion

Inclusion has always been our innate desire and passion; put simply, we want to be included- Included in the "life, liberty, and pursuit of happiness".

The entire conception and birth of the United States was due to a group of British citizens lack of inclusion, but was yet heavily taxed to help fund the government.

They had left Britain to colonize "for Britain" this new world in North America. But, the British government, through taxation, took their spoils and left them to fend for themselves; thus, gave birth to the term taxation without representation.

So, the colonist wrote a letter to Britain declaring their separation and forming their own government. The letter was called The Declaration of Independence.

But, most people miss a very important part of that declaration; at the very beginning.

Note what it says:

When in the course of human events it becomes necessary for one people to dissolve the political bands which have connected them with another and to assume among the powers of the earth, the separate and equal station to which the Laws of Nature and of Nature's God entitle them, a decent respect to the opinions of mankind requires that they should declare the causes which impel them to the separation.

In other words, these thirteen colonies came together and started a new world (the United States); it would still have taxation, but now with fair representation-a new sovereign nation that they created for themselves.

What they were saying, in essence, is that it is our right given us by our Creator to be treated justly, and politics was designed to give the people a voice; everyone is included, not just the rich. Everyone is supposed to be represented; thereby, the masses agree, in turn, to pay taxed as a means to take care of their states because now they were included.

They declared that the new nation shall have a government that shall be ruled by the governed-democracy. Democracy means that everyone is "included".

They further state that every man is due certain unalienable rights; among them are life, liberty, and the pursuit of happiness-every man was included; every white man that is.

The Constitution starts out by stated that it was written to form a more perfect union, but the problem was that all of its people were not "included"- the Negro was left out because he was seen as a piece of commodity own by some white man-some even among those that wrote the constitution.

It is called a Bill of Rights because it guarantees rights for all of its citizen.

So, hence, even from the United States birth, Negroes were not included, and now, over two hundred years later, he yet fights for inclusion.

I suspect that it is quite difficult and uncomfortable right now for white America to give the black man complete inclusion because if they do, they would be inadvertently admitting to its gravely wrongful acts, and egregious denial of even the constitution itself.

So, like the liberals, many of them stand with their heads down, shameful, but unwilling to right the wrong-hoping that the thorn in their side would just go away; that is the reason why you hear many of them saying that why don't y'all just get over it, or why won't y'all just move on. They quickly shout that that was the past.

But, our present state of being constantly reminds me of our past, therefore, the lynching, the rapes, the beatings, the non rights, the water hoses, the dogs, the police brutality are ever with me every day because the black man is yet denied inclusion over two hundred years later.

Even though most black people today are far removed from slavery, we still suffer from the ill effects of slavery; and most blacks of today were never a slave; their parents were not slaves, neither their grandparents. They were born in the United States, but still, right now, they are still treated as some of America's commodity that has lost some of its value.

Most often the only rights flashed before the black man is the Miranda rights that the police give him as they are arresting him, and the Miranda rights, are not really designed for the one that is being arrested; its purpose is of such notification to preserve the admissibility of the statements made by the one being arrested so that they can be admissible during further criminal proceedings-but, many times, just as his constitutional rights are overlooked, so is hi Miranda rights overlooked.

One of the most prominent ways that America has so effectively denied the black race inclusion was extracted from the slave era-the Black Driver-not a black man that drives a car, but a black man that was a slave that was in charge of all the other slaves on the plantation.

It was the black head slave that kept the Negro slaves in line; he dished out Mr. Charlie's punishment, and he was the one that was the middle person for the slave and the white slave owner.

Thus, we still have "drivers" now that try their best to pacify the black man to accept the non- inclusion state that he is in; of course they don't call them drivers now. Sometimes, they are black politicians and even a few black pastors that would have the black man to believe that all is well.

But, the black man still carries the status of a Negro, and he yet fights for inclusion in the United States and around the world.

It quietly resonates around the world that being black or any people of color is a crime or a taboo; So, the struggle for inclusion remain.

Martin Luther King said that he had a dream that one day little black boys and girls would walk down the streets holding hands with little white boys and girls. He didn't anticipate us adopting their callous ways. The dreamer's dream, then, becomes our nightmare, for we still suffer the same injustices, even though we can now drink from the same water fountain, and go through the front doors of businesses, and no longer have to sit in the back of the bus. Still, it is a far cry from Inclusion.

I suspect that Booker T. Washington knew this all along when he recommended that it was good for separation of blacks and whites. He said that we could co-mingle together, and be as together as the hand but as divided as the fingers. He suggested that blacks and whites could live together and apart at the same time.

He knew, even back then, that inclusion would always be illusive to the Negro, and be just a continuous illusion perpetrated by the American leaders under the guise of a constitution that was never intended to include the Negro.

Too, Marcus Garvey never believed that the Negro would ever truly experience inclusion in the United States, so he started the "go back to Africa" movement-specifically Liberia West Africa. Liberia had been colonized by ex-slaves. They started their own country where they would not have to fight for inclusion. Garvey concluded that Liberia would be a prime place for Black Nationalism.

For this reason Marcus Garvey, a Jamaican, created and organized the Universal Negro Improvement Association (UNIA); unlike NAACP organized by a white woman. The UNIA was to foster assistance for the Negro journeying back to Africa. Garvey bought a steamship and called it The Black Star Line to help Negroes move to Liberia.

All of our leaders in the past sought to be included in the American dream.

I wonder whether the Negro will ever leave his Negro status and be the black man that demands inclusion.

Chapter Nine

The winding road
of freedom

During my life time, I have discovered that freedom is anything but free, and equality is always a never ending fight to be fought. Freedom and equality remains a struggle for people of color, especially black people; who were once Negroes (white commodity) that are gradually easing into a state of their own blackness where they no longer want to be labelled an ex-commodity because as long as they are labelled as such, they will be treated as such.

With all of its ills and mistreatment of people of color, I still love America. Somewhere in our life, America has to come face to face with her own demons, and try as best as she can to right some of the gross injustices that has been perpetrated upon people that were different, or less fortunate than her masses-people that were tried and convicted because of the color of their skin while never ever considering the content of their character.

And, I wished that I could say that it is just a United States problem, but people of color in the United Kingdom and many other countries suffer from the ills of racism as well.

It is a continuous struggle. Our biggest challenge is for black people to release themselves from the shackles of slavery that was place upon their minds; for it matters little if one's body is free, but one's mind is still shackled.

Marcus Garvey said that though a man has been set free, he will remain a willing slave as long as he has the mind of a slave, for the body follows the path of the mind.

The problem with the slave's freedom in 1865 was that after the law was passed and the Thirteenth Amendment was instituted to free the slaves, Mr. Charlie just came and told the slaves that they were now free; but they had no training, no land, and no money, so what the slaves did was chose to remain with their slave owners under the same conditions-a Negro-Mr. Charlie's property-technically and legally free, but still a slave.

Thus, in order for the black man to pull off his Negro status he must walk within these 6 principals:

1. **The black race has to walk in FORGIVENESS and love.** We must love and forgive those that have perpetrated this mass gross of injustice placed upon us for over two hundred years. You will never truly forgive without the bands of love. Love is the only thing that makes true forgiveness possible. Unless the black man forgives those that enslaved him, he will never ever be truly free; for un-forgiveness is a powerful unrelenting shackle that binds much more than chains, for it shackles the mind and forces the individual to remain a Negro slave-still owned by the slave master. Forgiveness is the greatest weapon that the black man possesses, for it affords him the power and might to go forward. The reason why forgiveness is so powerful and moves even heaven is because one has to **choose** to forgive-even while one still remembers the offence and is yet hurting, and bruised, while the whelps of injustice is still freshly upon you. When you choose to forgive, you release the mental chains that keep you bound; that is why Jesus said for us to forgive our enemies. We must say, "I forgive you for lynching my brothers, for raping my mothers and sisters; I forgive you for denying me my constitutional unalienable rights of life, liberty, and the pursuit of happiness. I forgive you for tearing apart my family and selling some of us to the highest bidder. I forgive you for forcing me to sit at the back of the bus and making me give up my seat to someone whose skin is different from mine; I forgive you for treating me inferior to you and making me drink and sit in designated public places. I forgive you for the police brutality and humiliation, and for making your dogs bite me; I forgive you and love you still, for now I am ready to move forward in love-a love that cannot be legislated or manipulated. I forgive you even for all the indignities that you shall force upon me futuristically because I love you with a Godly kind of love. Now my mind becomes unshackled and I am released to walk in my destiny. Forgiveness and love allows the black man to live, perhaps, unlike he has ever lived before. Do not wait to forget the breach; God did not design us to forget. We remember all that has been done to us, but still we must choose to forgive; that is why it is a powerful Godly act!

2. **He has to stop referring to himself as any derivative of Negro-** Nigger, my Nigger, or any such term. When he refers to himself as such, he is saying that mentally, he still acknowledges that he is someone else's property-though he is free; the oxymoron-a free slave. The black man hasn't been a Negro (commodity) in over two hundred years, yet, so often he still refers to himself as such. Others will never see in you more than what you see in yourself. If you refer to yourself as someone's property, then you soon become someone's property. A host of entertainers use that Negro term so loosely and easily, like it is a term of endearment; so the youth, trying to immolate them, also slang the term around amongst their peers; not really understanding that they are acknowledging that they are some white man's property. To quit the life, you must also yield up the label, for as long as we wear the label, we are still but a slave-no doubt, a slave with stuff to foster the appearance of freedom.

3. **The black man must channel his economical power.** Black people spend over 1.1 trillion dollars annually in America, and spend 4% more annually than any other race. And, their spending is fast on its way to becoming 1.5 trillion annually which collectively should bring about much influence and clout amongst businesses and politicians. There are about three million black businesses in America. If you put all of that together, you will find that the black race, unlike the Negro, can demand some things and some changes because white America might not like black, but they surely love green. W. E. Dubois had it right when he said that black people have a common interest in the struggle for justice, equality, and freedom, therefore, they should work together. We must pool our money and resources and force a change; that is what happened in Montgomery Alabama bus boycott when Rosa Parks refused to give up her seat to a white man. Montgomery changed the bus seating for black people where they no longer had to sit in the back of the bus and give up their seat to white people. Montgomery didn't change because they had a conscious, or because they started loving black folk; no, they changed because those black people came together and decided that their money

was no longer going to support a racist bus system. They forced the Montgomery city bus system to change. Research says that when you calculate the dollar spent in our neighborhoods, it only stays in the black community for about six hours; which indicates to us that we make the money, we just take it across town or up town and give it back to the white business owners who oftentimes don't spend a dime in the black community. Note the time that the dollar spends in the community of other races: the dollar spends seventeen hours in the white community; twenty hours in the Jewish community, and thirty hours in the Asian community. See the vast difference. We must change and invest our money in us, and operate collectively to generate a better life for our children. If we spend our money at Coke, Cadillac, Mercedes, Honda, Chevrolet, Ford, Nike, Publix, Piggly Wiggly, or any designer store; we can demand change. Congress cannot legislate love, but our economical strength can profoundly persuade them to treat us fairly and with dignity. Black people spend four percent more money annually than any other race-even though most other races make more than them, and even though we sometimes live in ravaged neighborhoods and substandard houses-we're still anxious to spend our money and carry it off to build someone else's wealth. A prime example of this is when you look in the black community and you see a Mercedes or other expensive car parked in the governmental housing projects, or some other substandard house (a great part of their income is spent on a vehicle); Or they'll put five thousand dollars' worth of car rims on a seven hundred dollar car; this is the reason why most black folk die broke and leave their children nothing; which is one of the distinct differences between white folk and black folk. The masses of Black folk seem to live for "right now"-not fully concerning themselves with posterity-the wealth of their children. White America will always listen to your voice if you have economical strength.

4. **The black man must strengthen his political power.** He must play a part the political system, thereby, affecting the judicial system that enacts laws that sometimes foster systematic slavery. He must exercise his right to vote, particularly in local elections.

The right to vote was afforded the black man through blood, sweat and tears. When one has political power, the would be candidates that is running for a certain office will seek them out in order to get their vote. Voting is one avenue that black folks can use to enhance their quality of living, right some wrongs, and bring about a more qualitative life for their children, but it will never happen if we fail to vote. We must stand one our constitutional rights. It is the only way by which the black community can help change the system, thereby, destroying systematic slavery. Our adversary knows that voters have the power to greatly weaken him, so he does everything that he can to keep us away from the ballot box and making it difficult to go vote......ie, redistricting counties to lessen the black numbers in certain section, and seeing that the jails are disproportionately filled with black men, they take away their constitutional right to vote-despite the legislature taught the masses that the only way an American citizen can forfeit their rights as American citizens is by treason. Sun Tzu, in his book The Art of Ward, he teaches that you should watch your enemy closely before attacking; see what he tries to protect and guard the most, for therein lies his weaknesses. If the black race attacks the ballot and vote, we will weaken those that oppress us. Voting should be a priority of minorities.

5. **The black church, in our black neighborhoods, must become relevant again.** The church has made a metamorphosis from spiritual to flesh, from substance to shallow materialism; mainly, because the most difficult thing to do is to teach a man of his own spirituality when he dwells in a very substance based world. Churches have become inundated with feel good sermons that are saturated with motivational speeches that promise the listeners that God is about to give them more "stuff". Just as in the past, the black church and pastor must deal with the realities of what is happening right now in our neighborhoods-injustice, brutality, racism, non-inclusion, profiling etc. If we just preach about Daniel in the lion den, then, it becomes just a sermon on history. The pastors must bring Daniel's story to "today"; how do we escape our lion's dens in our streets, courtrooms, and in the justice system.

Many think that they escape our plight, and that things are different because they go out and join a white congregation, not realizing that they are but a token member. What affects one of us, affects all of us. It is a sin not to take care of your own. And, the flip side of this church relevance issue is that we have some churches that are so stuck in the past and what happened during the sixties until they cannot be relevant today, right now; they just relive yesterday over and over again, and fail to foster solutions for today. No, we mustn't forget what happened to us yesterday-the church bombings; the dog attack against the civil rights marchers, or the police brutality! For if we soon forget, it shall repeat itself, but we must face "today"-the issues that confronts us now; many are the same age old issues, but, none-the-less, still issues. Our churches are the best place to keep the movement going-seeing that black folks are a very spiritual people. Pastors who control the microphones have a distinct responsibility and duty to "say something" of relevance that's going to help our plight by opening our eyes. We already have enough entertainment. Let our sermons of change and betterment echo throughout the community during the week. Jesus didn't preach to make the people feel good; he preached for change; that's why he told the people that He came that they might have life and have it more abundantly. The church has to return to being a beacon in the community. Entertaining the masses simply pacifies them in their inequality, racist, and non-inclusive environment. Churches must pull off that "we're doing fine" attitude that they often cradle in their bosom while beaming with pride. It becomes a sad story when the church becomes so misguided and caught up in materialism just as the common man on the streets-thriving, but don't want to give anything back into the community where it stands. Is it not ludicrous to have more than two hundred thousand dollars in the bank, and yet refuse to change the riveting fading carpet on the floor because you don't want to disturb the saved money in the bank; that church faith is in their money in the bank and not in Jehovah that gave them the money. The church starts praising the gift more that the giver. It is sad and unfortunate, but that is the mindset that many pastors have to deal with today-the worshiping of Caesar's money. We have to change! The church is our last stand of hope, and I pray to God that the pastors and members of this new aged church will soon see it before we're all thrust back into the bitter upheavals of yesterday.

6. **Parenting the new generation.** We will always be looked upon as Negro and treated like somebody's property as long as we fail to be the parents that our children need. Our children can't break the Negro mindset by themselves. They don't need a friend; they need a parent! When we speak of parenting, we speak unequivocally of the mother and father in the home environment effectively enforcing practices that produce positive standards for their children, thereby birthing a healthy community. The community is simply a reflection of the state of parenting. I already know that perhaps many shall disagree with this statement, but today's black parenting skills were invaded and diluted by the white folk's rearing of their children, for we allowed the freedom of the white children's home to infiltrate our homes; so thus, the black child now oftentimes are emulating his white friends. Thus, is the reason why I stated previously that integration hurt the black family more than it helped black folks. Before our children started living amongst the white children and going to school with them, and seeing their blatant disrespect for their parents, they didn't dare talk back, or curse at their parents, or interrupt grown folk's conversation. No, they learned that from the white children. And, the black parents began adopting their parenting skills from the white parents. You can't expect little Johnny to be respectful at school when he is disrespectful at home. Black parents had no such thing in the home as "time out, or put your face against the wall". In the black home, there were consequences for a child getting out of their place, so parents have got to take back their homes. A child must be demanded to respect, honor, and the consequences of failing to do the right thing. We cannot get upset because the teachers won't allow our children to pray at school when we won't first pray at home. Another of the black parenting problem is babies are having babies and grandparents

are becoming grandparents at a much younger age, therefore, not really wanting to be a grandparents. Every black family needs a Madear-that grandmother that didn't play; that backed up the parents and put a whipping on your behind when you needed it. Parenting is the quintessential of the home and the bedrock of the community.

If black people continue to grossly fail in these five areas, 1.Continuing to refer to himself by any derivative of Negro 2. Continue to vacate or disregard of political power 3. Continue to disregard his economical power 4. Continue to remain an relevant church that fails to addresses the issues that is disproportionately plaguing us, they will remain and always be just a Negro who will remain to act like somebody else's property, though they are free-mentally a slave.

Parting words

Every time that I am referred to as Negro, or any derivative of Negro, I am thrust back to merely being a used commodity of the white man. The black man is never truly free as long as he is perceived as a Negro.

By inherent slave definition, Negro means to be not fully American, a second class citizen, if citizen at all; which is why the black man still struggles for civil rights, inclusion, and justice today.

The Negro has no country. He is too black to be American, and too American to be African-thus, his Americanized dilemma created by white America.

He was torn from Africa and violently thrusted into the abyss of "Negroism"-A man whose country never sees him as a man, but merely a piece of usable or useless property.

The black man's presence to the white man is a constant ugly reminder of his own unrighteous ways of injustice, and he realizes all to well that repercussions are soon to come from the mighty hands of Jehovah-The God that none can escape.

The black man is such an offence to white America because, like a child conceived out of adultery, he is a constant reminder of their sins and the horrors of their actions against an innocent race.

Our backs have been riddled with boroughs deepened by the white man's whip and planted with seeds of inferiority, servitude, and hate; a hate that is so pervasive and consuming until the black man subconsciously hates himself, even the very color of his own sun bath melanin rich skin-he is systematically trained to hate his own blackness-thus, he desperately tries to chemically change who he is, so he fries and colors his hair because Mr. and Mrs. Charlie's hair is straight and blond, so he wants his hair to look like theirs; he bleaches his skin so that he can look white, and he colors his eyes with eye contacts to capture the color of Mr. Charlie's eyes; all of this is done to look as non-black as he can.

But, there are a few black men that are waking up and beginning to walk in the fullness of whom they are and who they were supposed to be.

Dr. Martin Luther King said that no one can ride your back if you straighten up and stop bending over. I am simply echoing what has already been said, "Straighten up".

If you are tired of being somebody's Negro, then, stop being and acting like a Negro-somebody's property; stop referring to yourself or any other black person by any term deriving from Negro, for your words have power.

Forgive those that have wronged you, but you can't forgive them without loving them; and to do that, the black race have got to return to believing in something, a power that is greater than themselves; trust Jehovah to right the wrongs.

We must make church more than just a place to go to get our egos stroked, and told how we all are going to become rich tomorrow; no, church has to return to being the headquarters of the community where we hear from God and forge a greater union amongst us.

And, though it is deeply ingrained in my history, I am no longer anybody's Negro. I am now become freed in my body and mind.

As long as we choose to remain somebody's Negro, then true freedom and equality will continue to elude us.

I love this country and am an American through and through. I was born and raised here, and so was my mother and grandmother, straight down to perhaps many great great grandparent.

Our only quest is to make it the best that it can be for all people, of all nationalities, for America is the great melting pot of the world. We are passionate to make it a better place for our children and their children, both black and white, but we cannot do this divided and I am looked upon as a Negro

Judge me by the content of my character, rather than by the color of my skin, for I am deeper than the hue of my skin.

I am a free constitution abiding citizen of the United States of America, and I am now nobody's property, and never shall return to being somebody's Negro.

BLACK POETRY

Dr. Akeam A. Simmons

Ghetto Baby

Oh there you are
Ghetto star
Now with a ghetto baby
No man, little chance-maybe
You are by yourself again now
And don't even wonder how

You already knew this
Before he hollered that it's not his

You refuse to go anywhere
Love him right down to his curly hair

For you ghetto lady, never was life a breeze
To go through with any ease

He left you
No, he was never with you
He only wanted to use you
Then he was through with you
Now look at you
Left with another little you
That you promise won't be another you

Dog he is, left you pregnant
But you'll not forget him-you can't

He left a part of himself
You gave a part of yourself
Now all that is left
Is that from the two selves

You promise your baby that he'll not be in the system
And have to fight with them
And he'll not be like him
The father that left us on a whim
So hold your head up and never have your mental eyes close
Cause you don't want another dose
Of pain from those
Men you unwisely chose

For yourself and your baby you weep
And can't get no sleep
But you must become a lioness cause dogs always chase sheep
This one you decided to keep
But the many others you flushed to the deep
And tossed them to the graveyard's heap

The dog you must forgive
You got to if you want you and your baby to live
And your broken heart to heal

So get back in school
And refuse to be anybody's fool
And don't carry past baggage like a mule

When you and your baby make it out
And you finish with your thankful shout
Reach back and help another sister out

And don't judge all men like the dog you had
Cause all men are not bad
Some are over joyful in becoming a dad
And train a man from a lad

Respect yourself, when he says that if you love me you'll do this
Your reply is if you love me, you won't ask me to do this

Respect yourself and demand the respect of others
If he cannot respect you, don't even bother
Cause he probably won't make a good husband or a good father

Color Matters

You say color doesn't matter
Then why do I remain the same and your pockets get fatter

You say color doesn't matter
Then why refer to me as the less and you the batter

You say color doesn't matter
Then give me my promised land so I can be a better father

You say color doesn't matter
Then why is your condition getting better and mind sadder

You say color doesn't matter
Then why do you get nervous when you see my people gather

You say color doesn't matter
Then why do you treat me like the joker or the mad hatter

You say that color doesn't matter
Then you show me that it does in every day matter

Yes color does matter

You deny me my rights because of my color
You give me injustice because of my color
You profile me because of my color
You stigmatize me because of my color
You criticize me because of my color
You ostracize me because of my color
You fear me because of my color
You wrote me off because of my color

Yes...........Yes
Color does matter or how else can I explain my strength to survive

Slave

I am but a slave
Degrees of freedom I am gave
But still but a slave

Sometimes beaten for how I behave
The way of my life has already been pave
Unless someone searches for the me to save

This slavery goes pass the color of my skin
Or where I come from or where I have been

It systematically steals my heart
And forces my soul and spirit to come apart
But all of this I must sort
If ever I want a new start

Whipped be I
I holler up to the sky
Until all I can do is sigh
And feel my body about to die

But they'll never brake what mama put in me
So over and over I flee
If not but in my dreams of me
Wondering the streets s free

They may enslave my body
But my soul is forever free
Cause that's the way God designed it to be

So every night when I lay down
I take a trip into some town
And dance all night with some lady in a pretty gown
Where no man looks at me and frown

When I awake
I realize it's fake
I am still but a slave for goodness sake

But then I smile
Cause nights coming in awhile
When I'll travel for miles
Without ever leaving my bed pile

Every night in my dreams I am free
To truly be me
Nobody's slave just free to once be me
Free as I can be

Change

You are what you were
And you will always be
What you have always been

To look at your ancestors
Is to look into your life's mirror
To change who I will become
I must change who I am right now
Change is difficult and painful
But I realize that there is significant purpose to my pain
Change will not become complete without pain
Pain, like fear, is a gift to me
A warning system to alert and alarm
For needed positive change
I must never allow myself to become dull
And numb to my pain and fear
For in so doing, I limit myself to rise no higher than my ancestors
And close the doors to any positive change for me and my offspring

Man

Man's only hope is his relationship to his creator. The only morality that man will ever come to have and sustain is connected to his creator. There is no "moral" fiber in him without God. He flows aimlessly as the beast, driven only by pain and pleasure. When he doesn't know God, he doesn't know himself-thus is the all-consuming paradox of Hu-man.

He's always with himself but yet he doesn't know himself, not even a little. He dwells outside of himself.

His means are his end; therefore, his perception is always his reality. He only sees what he expects to see; thus, his vision is always clouded if he has any at all.

Born into the world naked without an owner's manual, he is clueless of his true "self". He is a result of nurture and nature.

Man has watched others and learned to be a brute beast lacking the nature of God-Jehovah. He sees, so he becomes; he becomes, so he sees. The cycle is infinite. That's why he fears what he doesn't understand, and is uncomfortable with that for which he finds different. Oh wretched man is he.

No wonder Jehovah asked Adam, "Who told you that you were naked?"

Let Me Live

Why won't they just leave me alone
All of us from time to time have done wrong
But it's not about something under my breath I'll moan
Cause all of us have shameful skeletons in our home

Just let me live, even after I've messed up
Just let me live; there's already enough pain in my cup
Make me not a monster because of where I sup
I have fallen but I can get back up
Just let me alone while I lick my wounds like a little pup

Be patient with me because your time is sure to come
Then, I'll leave you alone and play like I am dumb
And not know that you have fallen and become undone

Just let me live my life
Without your added drama and strife
In secret your month cutting me like a knife
Like the scorn of a betrayed wife

Just let me live and you will soon see where I am coming from
In my weakness, in my brokenness, I need the love of a mom
To help rebuild my soul from where it has come

Leave me alone; stop talking about me and pray for me
I will soon be alright; you'll see
If you'll just give me time to become free
From the demons that haunt me

Just let me live; I didn't come here to stay long
Some day as appointed I'll be going home
Just leave me alone
While I wrestle with this private hell I've been thrown

And even though I am the only one to blame
Please be careful not to scandalize my name
And cause me to walk with my head down in shame

Just let me live, and I'll come out of this stronger
Where my old demons won't torture me any longer
And my thirst for righteousness will be my main hunger

Just……..Let……..Me………Live

Um Not Colored

I bleach my skin and color blond my hair
But I am still colored they say with a stare
I ignore and keep bleaching cause white I still dare
Cause Negroes have too much to care

I change my name and even my eye color to be like
But when I look in the mirror I see um still not white
And when I go to public places um still not treated right
But I'll keep trying until I become white
To change my black forsaken plight

When they move away trying to separate from me
I move too hoping that my whiteness their soon see
Um black on the outside but white on the inside, from me don't flee
As long as um black in a white world, I can never be truly free
I try to hide my outside blackness with inside whiteness so to agree
So the white world would be happy with me

My hair is not nappy and curly no more
It's straight like theirs but the chemicals made my head sore
Even with my straight hair and bleached skin which I adore
They still keep closed opportunities' door

Even-though my mama and daddy is black, um still white
Give me a cone head and a white sheet so I can burn a cross tonight
Cause I am white
I already stabbed many Negroes in the back
And think that ain't none of them too bright
Cause um white

I go to church with them too
And worship God like they do
Don't take all that jumping and shouting like the Negroes do
Silently sit in church for an hour or few
Then leave and go hang a Negro or two

No, I ain't colored no more
I've seen my daddy constantly knocked to the floor
And my mama scrub floors until her knees were callous and sore
My brothers and sisters forced to walk through the back door
They just became a white man's whore

But, in spite of all that I try
All I can do is but cry
Cause with my bleached skin, my purchased nose and my hair fry
I am still colored black, and will be colored black till the day I die

Now I accept and love my beautiful black skin that I see
And realize that there is royalty in me
In spite of the slave that they tried to create me to be
I am black and proud and also free
For they can't enslave a man that learns who he was supposed to be

My Grand Child

God knew that in older age sometimes I would need a smile
So he set aside drops of his sunshine and called them grandchild
To keep me from growing old bitter and foul

And even though you will grow up, you'll always be my grandchild
So expect me to be in your life for a good long while
To help you succeed by the inch or by the mile

I held you when you were only a little bigger than the palm of my hand
I watched you make mud pies and play in the sand
And hope and pray that you'll be an asset to all man
To help mold and make this world a better land

So when you cry, I will wipe away your tears
Because some day you will wipe away my tears
I'll make you strong and silence your fears
Because some day you will make me strong and silence my fears

I can always see a little of me in you
But I guess that is what all grandparents do
You drive away my days that's blue
Just by your presence and you just being you

You're such a wonderful ball of energy
Jumping about here and there seeing what you can see
Far too much energy for me
So I'll just wait until you tire and find my lap to fall asleep

While you dream, I hold you close
The best grandchild I constantly boast
And always remember grandparents love you most

Now, I hold your hand to sturdy you
Someday you'll hold my hand to sturdy me too

Whatever life throws our way
We'll make it the brighter day
So when you need a hug or a smile, just find grandparent's stay
And there you'll find how to ease your hurts and troubles away

My Flesh

It be most difficult to face
Knowing fully my rightful place
But still having to give my rights my chase
Because my heart has no base
So live I under the secrecy of fleshly disgrace

My flesh is miserable over bearing heat
That my soul cannot easily meet
To sooth this heart's unhappy broken rhythmic beat
Of deep passionate desires from holy feats

Who am I
I have forgotten me, but how and why
For the painted on smile does not satisfy
My flesh wreaks, my emotions defy
Having experienced a degree of death even before I die

Oh sooth me threw oh slumbering night that hides from day
The heat that only the chosen can slay
I weep, I moan, my soul's dismay
To conquer these feelings I hide that still betray
I must undoubtedly faithfully pray
And par......and pray......and pray

Mama's Little Boy

I watch you try hard to accept daddy's death
While you're constantly plagued with failing health
We try to comfort you but you still feel that you're by yourself

I am a grown man now
But the little boy in me is crying, screaming how
As tears swell in my eyes and race down my brow

You use to could make everything all right
So how do I put back in you the will to fight
Because your little boy in me has come to fright

Mama can you hear me; I am scared of the night
But now, you're not able to come turn on my night light
The man outside tries to be strong, but the little boy inside is contrite
Hoping and praying with all of my might
That dear mama won't succumb and die in this night

And though I live so very far away
You're in my heart to stay
Your little boy on the inside doesn't know how to say
But the man on the outside must convey
The hurt and pain experienced by both of them every day

I try to act for mama like I am fine
But her little boy is running out of time
A am scared that mama's light will soon not shine
And her little boy will be left behind
Never, ever again to be fine

Little boys are never ready for their mamas to die
But I see death creeping upon her, and all I can do is cry

As I use to, I want to hold onto her dress tail
Allowing the man in the little boy to slowly unveil
Thank you mama; thank you mama; over and over I wail
As my tears gather in eternity's well
But for mama, this man boy must not derail
It is appointed upon men once for death to see
So painfully I accept the inevitable, mama will soon leave me
Because that's how our God designed it to be
I am ashamed that I waited until death got close before I could see
Just how much mama means to me
Even though I am a man, her insecure little boy is still inside of me
Weeping for mama's eyes to continue to see

Fly

You will always fly
If you pay the one that owns the sky
And never wonder and try to reason why
He alone can own the sky
And never die

So fly and fly as long as you can fly
Surrounded by the one that owns the earth and the sky
Until he bids you it is time for you to die
And leave another for you to cry

Enter a world where angels fly
And nobody over there ever die
Or bid anyone forever goodbye
Just fly and fly

Black Me

My skin is black because the sun rested upon my fathers
And cleaved to my mothers
My blackness pushes justice for me farther
And causes love among my colorless brothers to falter

My God took the clay from the earth and colored me
He curled my hair and smoothed my skin gallantly
That I might be free
To race with the sun shining on me

And though injustice reign because of the color of my skin
They cannot erase that my father is first from whence God begin
Many a things come and go but my blackness is not a trend
Though sometimes it's mixed with others and forced to blend
Still I am black through and through from start to end

God took the best of Him and made the best of me
So if you look past my color and see me
You'll see God's best on display in me
And all of His marvelous wonders for all to see

From mother earth I was born
From my father's land I was torn
To the slave masters I was joined
And cruelty of my situation caused me to mourn

Oh but my masters couldn't steal my pride
And my royalty they could not hide
For all the cruelty they threw at me I took in stride
Because constantly to the God of heaven I confide

Daily they try to make me forget my past
But my future shoots forth from my past
And the king in me enables me to stand fast
Break away the image of me that they try to cast

My color is not a curse
Even though over the years this they tried to nurse
Trying to make me feel my color is a curse
But I am the seed of royalty because God made me first

So now I'll lift my head up and walk proudly
Shouting to the world of whose I am out loudly
Because my God took the best of Him and made the best of me

My Daddy's Eyes

I look in the mirror and I see
My daddy's eyes staring back at me
Oh how can this be
When yesterday he refused to raise me
And teach me what a man I should be

My daddy's eyes

I don't see how
He could stare back at me now
When over the years he refused me even the milk of a cow

My Daddy's eyes

But there he is looking back at me
Smiling a little can't you see
Proud of what he sees in me
Of what mama along reared me to be
My daddy's eyes

To my high school graduation
He had no invitation
Because he wasn't there helping during my struggling situations
Helping mama protect me from the world's annihilation

My daddy's eyes

How dare he show up in my mirror
Secretly beckoning to become dearer
While death eases upon him ever so nearer
But there he is staring back at me in my mirror

My daddy's eyes

Forgiveness he screams out to me silently
I scream back amongst shattered glass now I am free
And mama has long gone home peaceably
Only after raising me to be the man that I should be
My daddy's eyes

I look down upon the floor at the broken glass
And I still see through one of the pieces his cast
Staring back at me with tears over the years he has mask
I pick up a piece and I see tears flowing down my daddy's face
Knowing full well of all the pain and hurt he can't erase

My daddy's eyes

But to be the man that I should be
I have got to forgive him for failing to be the man he should be
I forgive you daddy for forsaking mama and me
And thanks for looking in on me
Even if it was only through the mirror that I could see
The pain filled eyes begging forgiveness from me

My daddy's eyes

In Me

I watch and guard against my enemy
And protect myself from where he will be
Then I realize that my real enemy
Is locked up inside of me

Oh you can't see my real enemy
For he hides deep inside of me
Quenching the things that I should be
And trying hard to disrupt my destiny

In me resides royalty
Between faithfulness and specialty
Gallops my reality
Of things of hopes that I should be

In me in my bosom rests kings
Alluring queens to come to honor and sing
Of the holy of holies signature ring
On things so utterly wonderful to cling

In me I see what some refuse to see
The greater part of me
A resting giant waiting to be
The uniqueness of just being me

The prisons built by me for me
Cannot hold the real me
Who sores the skies ever so glee
And pays the price to be continuously free

You In Me

I look deep into your eyes and wonder what you see
And hope that you'll always see me
And what I am supposed to be
In your life for you to see

So gentle, so fragile, so innocent
Would that I could save you from life's lament
And give you virtue before innocents spent

From God you were sent
To demonstrate His holy establishment
Life will sometimes be broke, bruised and bent
You'll learn that this is how mere mortals pay life's rent

Go on coo and giggle and let your eyes be a glazed
Crawl and find things by which you are amazed

I stare at you while you sleep
And wonder how can I keep
One that is in my heart so deep
From troubles that will come in heaps
And heart break that will make you weep

I hear your every cry
And rush Iike I can fly
To wipe away your tears
And silence all of our fears

If I could just hide you
From the evils that people do
And the pain that comes from them lying to you

I promise I'll shield you as best I can from any hurt
Until in one of our faces they throw some dirt

Just take it one step at a time
And I know that you'll be fine
So when Gabriel's horn chimes
You'll be ready to cross that eternal line

Dear God

Give me the wisdom to lay down my sword
When the battle is over
Give me the courage to stand still and wait on you
After I have fought a good fight
Give me peace of mind
When the end is not what I expected it to be
Give me strength to go forward
When my soul wants to quit
And teach me the difference between
Real victory and real defeat

Printed in the United States
By Bookmasters